READING UNBOUND

WHY KIDS NEED TO READ WHAT THEY WANT—AND WHY WE SHOULD LET THEM

Jeffrey D. Wilhelm and Michael W. Smith

with Sharon Fransen

■ SCHOLASTIC

New York • Toronto • London • Auckland • Sydney
Mexico City • New Delhi • Hong Kong • Buenos Aires

2/14

D0690947

DEDICATION

From Jeff ~ *To Jasmine Marie Wilhelm*

My lovely and book-loving daughter and one of my great teachers

And to all the students with whom I've read, responded,
and learned over the last 32 years of teaching

From Michael ~ *To Gabrielle Rita White*

Granddaughter extraordinaire and the biggest lover of stories I know

Cover Designer: Scott Davis; Illustration: Shauna Lynn Panczyszyn; Photo: © Golden Pixels LLC/Alamy
Editor: Lois Bridges
Copy/Production Editor: Danny Miller
Interior Designer: Sarah Morrow
Copyright © 2014 by Jeffrey D. Wilhelm and Michael W. Smith
All rights reserved. Published by Scholastic Inc.
Printed in the U.S.A.
ISBN: 978-0-545-14780-4

1 2 3 4 5 6 7 8 9 10 40 21 20 19 18 17 16 15 14

CONTENTS

ACKNOWLEDGMENTS 4

PART 1 — THE NATURE AND VARIETY OF READING PLEASURES

Chapter 1   The Importance of Reading for Pleasure 5

Chapter 2   Reading Pleasure: Taking a Closer Look 14

Chapter 3   Play Pleasure: "I Just Get This Joy Reading" 30

Chapter 4   Work Pleasure: "This Is It!" 48

Chapter 5   Intellectual Pleasure: "It's Like Being a Detective Almost" 67

Chapter 6   Social Pleasure: "All My Friends Were Telling Me I Had to Read This" 85

PART 2 — THE PARTICULAR PLEASURES OF POPULAR GENRES

Chapter 7   Readers of the Heart: Getting Carried Away by Romances 101

Chapter 8   The Lure of Immortality: Going Batty for Vampire Novels 122

Chapter 9   The Call of Horror: Containing What's in the Dark Shadows 142

Chapter 10   Thinking the Unthinkable: Looking for Answers in Dystopian Fiction 152

Chapter 11   The Harry Potter Phenomenon: The Power of Imagination 166

Chapter 12   Where Do We Go From Here? 180

REFERENCES 187

ACKNOWLEDGMENTS

Jeff and Michael would first like to thank the good people at Scholastic who have been so supportive of (and patient with) us as we've worked on this book. We express our gratitude to Kyle Good, Senior Vice President of Scholastic Corporate Communication, for her immediate support—both encouragement and funding—that helped launch our research. A very special thanks goes to Lois Bridges for her encouragement, expert advice, and editing. Lois has been a real champion for the book and we appreciate all of her efforts on our behalf. And we thank our production and copy editor Danny Miller for his always brilliant work, as well as our book design team— Director of Art Jaime Lucero for the stunning cover (with invaluable guidance from Senior Vice President Patrick Daley!) and Sarah Morrow for her graceful, playful book design. Now, as we release the book into the world, we are grateful for Tyler Reed's expert guidance. We'd also like to thank James Earl Davis, who was serving as Interim Dean of Temple University's College of Education as we worked on this project, for providing support for our research assistant Sharon Fransen. Sharon did more to guide our thinking than any research assistant ever known! Peter Rabinowitz provided helpful feedback on our theoretical background and Jon-Philip Imbrenda did a very smart and very careful reading of the whole book. Sandra Abrams suggested that we might find Dewey's *Interest and Effort in Education* generative. She was certainly right.

Jeff wants to give a blue ribbon salute to his research assistants during our data collection, visiting BSWP fellows Erika Boas and Theresa Street, both for their work and their great enthusiasm for this project. Thanks also go to Diane Williams and Jasmine Wilhelm for their help in identifying informants, as well as to Sarah Veigel and Andrew Porter. Of course, Jeff is always grateful to his colleague Jim Fredricksen for his insightful advice and to all of the Boise State Writing Project fellows who responded to ideas and drafts. A special thanks to Jungian analyst Scott Hyder for responding to data and lending his expertise and sharing his work about vampires and horror. Jeff was also hugely helped in his thinking by the work of Clifford Mayes and Ruth Vinz. Of course, thanks and gratitude always go to Jeff's wife Peggy Jo Wilhelm, and to his daughter Fiona Luray, and to all the supportive colleagues and teachers and National Writing Project fellows and directors with whom Jeff has worked over the years.

Michael would like to thank his colleagues in the College of Education, especially those in the Department of Teaching and Learning, who make Temple such a personally and intellectually enriching place to work. David Devenney, Michael's Department Manager, and his staff of Gwen Miller, Pamela James, and Mary Vesey kept things running smoothly, which made finding time to write so much easier. Michael's mentor, George Hillocks, Jr., and his colleagues and friends from the University of Chicago, are always in his head as he writes. And his wife Karen Flynn and daughters Catherine and Rachel are always in his heart.

Sharon would like to thank Michael and Jeff for inviting her to help with this study and book. She found the experience to be tremendous from start to finish, and she has been honored to work for and with these two accomplished researchers/writers. Sharon also thanks her husband Jeff Landis for his encouragement, as well as her daughters Kate and Hannah for their love. This book only makes her more grateful for the pleasure they take in reading.

CHAPTER 1

The Importance of Reading for Pleasure

When Jeff was small, even before he could go to school, he remembers that every night he and his brother would sit on opposite armrests of their dad's big brown recliner as he read the sports page. They'd ask him to read them the headlines and then to explain something about the articles. After a bit they'd go visit their mom in her green revolving chair and snuggle in on opposite hips. Their mom would read them picture books. Jeff's favorite was *Best Friends for Frances* by Russell Hoban (possibly foreshadowing his going to the University of Wisconsin where he became a Badger himself). He loved how Frances dealt with problems with such aplomb and he tried to imitate her. He remembers once when a friend was being mean to him that he quoted Frances from that book, asking his friend: "Do you want to be friends, or do you want to have to be careful?" He appreciated Frances all the more when his friend didn't know what to say and started being nicer.

One of Michael's earliest memories is of the first time he took a book out of the library using his own library card. Though it was 1961, he can still see it vividly: the blue cardboard and grey metal rectangle with embossed numbers. The book: Syd Hoff's *Albert the Albatross*. As he entered his house, book in hand, his father asked him if he wanted to play cribbage, a nightly ritual the two of them had. But not that night. "No, Dad," Michael responded. "I think I'll just curl up in bed with a good book instead." And that he did for the first of many, many times.

Much more recently, Jeff was enjoying his monthly book club meeting. The conversation had been spirited and the book, the YA novel *Feed* by M.T. Anderson, had inspired a deep consideration of the role of technology in our lives and where it might be leading us. Towards the end of the evening, his dear friend Wita, a professor from Poland, brought up her monthly question: "But gentle readers, I must ask: Is this *literature?*" Gregor maintained that books written for teenagers couldn't possibly be literature. Jeff insisted that literature or literariness was not a quality of books, but of the reader's transaction with a book, and for him *Feed* was literature. Gemma said that the work was literature because her reading had moved and stretched her and because she had intensely enjoyed reading it. Mark said that this was precisely why it could not be considered literature! Literature was certainly not something to be enjoyed! And everyone laughed.

Not long ago Michael was at his granddaughter Gabrielle's karate class, reading a dissertation. The woman sitting next to him leaned over and said, "A dissertation, huh? My dad was a professor. I remember his carrying them around with him when he was ferrying us from place to place."

Michael had noticed that she was reading as well and asked, "And how about you? What are you reading?"

"Tripe," she responded. "Just a mystery." She then proceeded to point to her three sons, one on the mat with Gabrielle, the other two with her. "My sons are all on the autism spectrum," she said. "Sometimes I need a break and reading stuff like this gives me one," and with that she returned to her book.

As our stories make clear, while reading provides readers great pleasures, some reading experiences are marginalized, often by the readers themselves. The purpose of this book is to see what we can learn about the nature and variety of the pleasures kids take in their out-of-school reading and to make the case that rather than marginalizing reading pleasures, we should all think harder and in more complex ways about them and about how to promote and leverage these pleasures.

The Personal and Cultural Benefits of Literacy

Why are the pleasures of reading so neglected? Perhaps it's because we tend to focus instead on its power. Indeed, literacy is perhaps humanity's greatest achievement. Reading is certainly one of our most significant and complex cognitive acts, requiring the integration of many areas of the brain and of many separate capacities—vision, hearing, the ability to synthesize information, and much more. Reading is certainly necessary to navigate modern life, to function as an informed democratic citizen, to work in a knowledge economy. Using the Internet, multimodal and multimedia though it is, nonetheless requires significant reading. Being informed, especially about nuanced and complex issues, requires deep reading.

Literacy is essential not only to accessing information and staying up to date, it is also essential to doing work in the world. As President Obama exclaimed in a speech to the American Library Association:

> In this new economy, teaching our kids just enough so that they can get through Dick and Jane isn't going to cut it. Over the [next] ten years, the average literacy required for all American occupations is projected to rise by 14%. It's not enough just to recognize the words on the page anymore—the kind of literacy necessary for 21st century employment requires detailed understanding and complex comprehension.

Jobs for the Future, an organization dedicated to providing "career advancement for those struggling to succeed in today's economy," bases its work on the recognition "that jobs that pay family-sustaining wages" require "large and growing literacy needs." In short, jobs that require fuller literacy skills are increasing steadily while jobs requiring only routine manual skills are just as steadily decreasing. Certainly these trajectories introduce a dilemma to schools as the skills that are easiest to teach and test are also the ones that are easiest to digitize, automatize, robotize, and outsource. That's why the new generation of standards and assessments being implemented throughout all developed nations and embodied in the Common Core State Standards movement in the United States foregrounds the effort towards a literacy that encompasses problem-solving and higher-order thinking.

Literacy is important not only to an individual's success but also to the ultimate success of the entire culture. Diamond (1999), in his seminal work *Guns, Germs, and Steel*, highlights literacy as an essential element of cultural success and as a contributing factor in historical conquests. This theory explains in large part why Europeans sailed to the Americas and colonized them, instead of the highly successful societies in America sailing to Europe and colonizing the Europeans. In short, it's clear that at this time in history, we need to be able to read deeply a wide variety of texts, including multimedia texts, to be considered literate, to engage in modern life, and to address modern problems.

But it's not just the ability to read that's important, at least according to some thinkers. Hirsch (1987) argues influentially that people need to be culturally literate, that is, that they have to "possess the basic information needed to thrive in the modern world" (p. xiii).

Moreover, as the stories with which we began suggest, reading is not just cognitive. Reading is also deeply psychological and can engage our emotions and our spiritual impulses. Indeed, Nussbaum (1990) argues that "certain truths about human life can only be fittingly and accurately stated in the language and forms characteristic of the narrative artist" (p. 5). Currie (2013) notes that it's a commonplace belief that reading great literature makes us better people. Tatum's (2009) notion of textual lineages is based on his belief in the power of literature to transform lives.

We obviously recognize the power of reading. Indeed, we have dedicated our professional careers as teachers and researchers to understanding reading and readers and to helping teachers promote students' engaged and increasingly competent reading. But even if you believe strongly in the power of reading, you still have to recognize that all reading may not be equally powerful. Some forms of literacy may be more useful than others in allowing you to work and achieve success in the world. Some may more clearly mark you as culturally literate than others. Some may provide the means of developing your full human potential, while others may lead you in other less savory directions.

As a consequence, there's an ongoing cultural debate about which texts should be read and which ones should be avoided. The debate engages parents, other interested adults, policy makers, and of course, educators—from curriculum writers to classroom teachers. And even when there's agreement about the benefits a certain kind of text might offer, there's plenty of debate about how and when readers can best experience those benefits. Such debates can become quite intense. Teachers, parents, and cultural commentators from all political backgrounds often feel passionately about what our young people should read—both inside and outside of school.

In our own teaching careers, we've been engaged in this debate on many levels. On parent-teacher nights, attentive parents regularly worried aloud, often passionately, about their child's reading of fantasy, vampire novels, series books, and the like. Often they disapproved of the books their children were reading and even seemed to fear them. Almost always they asked how they could get their kids to read something else, something more useful, more prestigious, or better for them.

Sometimes parental disapproval leads to controversy that touches on censorship issues. Jeff was in the news for a short while for teaching *The Witch of Blackbird Pond* by Elizabeth George Speare, a Newbery Award-winning book that a group of parents singled out for being about witchcraft. (For the record, it's not about witchcraft, but about a young woman unjustly accused of being a witch.) The gist of the parents' argument was that reading this book was bad for their children, would stunt their growth, disturb them, erode their ethical sensibilities, and perhaps make them question their religious traditions.

The issue also came up in the context of the free reading our students did. Parents often called to complain about the books their children were reading, and it did no good to argue that the initiative was a "free choice" program—that the students were reading what they chose to read, and that allowing choice was designed to help them *become* readers as a foundation for improving as readers. It got to the point that Jeff had a bookshelf behind his desk with a sign that read "Parental Permission Required." (As you might guess, these books often became the most popular books in his classroom!)

Some of the books our kids read made us uneasy, too. But we saw many a reluctant or struggling reader become passionate about a series of fantasy books or about a horror author. We saw kids who were reluctant to read in class surreptitiously trading edgy Chris Crutcher novels.

So we started to ask: Might kids gravitate to the kinds of texts they need? Might they experience a deep fulfillment that we don't completely understand when they read those books? Might passionate readers of marginalized texts—those books that many parents and teachers disapprove of at some level—be choosing books that help them build on and develop new interests, become competent in new ways, and grow beyond their current selves? And then we thought: Why not ask young people directly what they get from their reading of such texts? Why not ask them how they experience and use them? And so we did.

This book is about the answers we received. In Part 1, we'll engage in an in-depth exploration of the nature and variety of the pleasures avid adolescent readers take in their out-of-school reading. In Part 2, we'll continue with a more precise focus on the pleasures and psychological satisfactions that committed readers of particular genres experience, focusing on the popular genres of romance, vampire stories, horror, dystopian fiction, and fantasy—texts that are often marginalized or dismissed by teachers and other adults. We'll conclude by sharing some ideas for how we can make reading for pleasure more central to the work we do in and out of schools to promote reading and literacy, and by exploring what benefits might accrue if we do so.

Spoiler alert: What we found is that the young people to whom we spoke were remarkably articulate about the benefits they received and the pleasures they experienced from their reading, often of books dismissed by some as "tripe," "junk," "pulp," "pap," or "trash." Their testimonies challenge those who reject books that are enjoyed by the masses—either youth or adults—based on the suspicion that these wildly popular books cannot provide a high quality or enriching reading experience.

In her article "Reading Is Not Eating" (1986), Janice A. Radway argues that such texts are comforting to their readers. This comfort, she contends, is not regarded as something of value. Instead the charge so often leveled at mass-produced literature is that it is not simply bad, nor even worthless, but that it is "capable of degrading, indeed, of corrupting those who enjoy it." This charge, in turn, "is based on the further assumption that similar and simple texts fail to engage readers in creative, productive response to thoughts and ideas that challenge or call their own into question." The reading experience of such books is characterized "by its passivity, by its complacency, and by its ability to promote the illusion that all is well" (p. 7).

Radway's own research in *Reading the Romance* (1988) demonstrates that such charges may be unfounded. She found that "some romance reading at least manages to help women address and even minimally transform the conditions of their daily existence" (p. 8). In other words, readers are not passive, but active and often transformative in the ways they transact with texts and use them. Society has, she argues, "failed to detect the essential complexity that can characterize the interaction between people and mass-produced culture" (p. 9)—including, we would argue, popular books.

It seems to us that discussions about reading revolve mostly around the WHAT instead of the WHY and the HOW. Both our cultural conversations and most investigations of popular culture are focused on the texts or objects of popular culture—a culture that we regard as known and fixed. This notion that readers submit to and consume cultural artifacts, rather than adapt and make them their own, is at odds with contemporary reading research and literary theory. The reader, we know from the work of Louise Rosenblatt (1978) and a host of other reader-response theorists and researchers, can accept, adapt, resist, and transform the meanings created in these transactions.

In "Reading Books, Great or Otherwise," Katha Pollitt (1991) writes:

> *Why, ask yourself, is everyone so hot under the collar about what to put on the required-reading shelf? It is because while we have been arguing so fiercely about which books make the best medicine, the patient has been slipping deeper and deeper into a coma. (p. 4)*

Pollitt asks us to imagine a country where reading is a popular voluntary activity, where people give books for presents, adults read for themselves and to their children, and schools are filled with attractive libraries so that students can read some books together, but also many books on their own. In such an environment, students would create their own identities as readers and learners. Pollitt writes:

> *In that country of real readers—voluntary, active, self-determined readers—a debate like the current one over the canon would not be taking place. Or if it did, it would be as a kind of parlor game: What books would you take with you to a desert island? Everyone would know that the top-ten list was merely a tiny fraction of the books one would read in a lifetime. (p. 34)*

We think Pollitt makes an excellent point. To extend her argument, we think that home and school should be places where readers are nurtured, supported, and assisted to create their own active reading lives, connected to their own life journeys. This is the only way in which students will become lifelong readers.

But what if those journeys don't lead readers to the culture's literary masterpieces? In many a department meeting we've heard something like the following: "But if they don't read Shakespeare [or Chaucer or Melville or Hawthorne] in school, then they will never read him." Our interpretation: "Because of the texts we choose and the ways we teach those texts, we're likely to ruin reading for students so that they'll never go to a Shakespeare play much less read one as an adult. That's why they have to read it now."

We question what being assigned ten or even a hundred well-chosen books throughout one's schooling will do for students. First, there is the assumption that students are reading the books that they are assigned. We know from our own research that this is highly doubtful. In one high school classroom during our *Reading Don't Fix No Chevys* study (2002), an examination of the literate life of young men both in and out of school, we identified 30 different strategies for making the teacher think you were reading a book that you were not actually reading. These strategies included techniques like indiscriminately moving a large bookmark throughout the book (like your teacher is paying attention to that!), going through the book and randomly highlighting passages or putting in sticky notes, going to sparknotes.com or foolyourteacher.com and coming up with a question to ask (asking the teacher such a question before class started, many students thought, could circumvent planned quizzes), acting really grateful when the teacher answered the question (*oh, now I get it!*), watching video versions with friends in informal video clubs, forming study groups based merely on readings of a summary, chipping in to pay one person to read the book and mentor you, and on and on. This was true even—and maybe especially— among honors and AP students. The takeaway: What were the kids learning? Not how to read. Not about the great themes of life and literature. Not about how texts work and can enliven and enrich us. They were basically learning how to cheat. This resonates with thinking about "opportunity to learn". Kids learn exactly what they have the opportunity to learn. The problem is that often we think we are offering one opportunity and they are seizing, for their own reasons, on entirely different opportunities.

Further, even if a student made an honest attempt to read the hundred well-chosen books, that doesn't mean he or she would enjoy, understand, or reflect upon them in any meaningful way. If you are not a reader with an independent reading life, then it's tough going to experience and remember some of these very challenging books.

A thought experiment: Imagine yourself on a crowded beach. Picture the people sitting on their beach chairs. What are they doing? Some are dozing. Some are staring at the ocean. Some are just working on their tans. But, at least in our minds' eyes, many are reading. But none of them are reading any of the hundred books or so that would be on a typical recommended reading list. We wouldn't be either. If we are honest with ourselves as readers, we have to admit that we read a wide variety of texts for a wide variety of reasons. But at the core of it, we read because we take pleasure in doing so.

THE PREREQUISITE POWER OF PLEASURE

When we began this study, we knew that pleasure would be an important consideration. But we had no idea how varied and powerful the notion of pleasure would be.

Following the lead of reader response theorists, both of us have long argued (Wilhelm, 2008; Rabinowitz & Smith, 1998) that thinking about literature requires thinking about more than the text itself. We also have to consider the experience a reader has with a text. If the power and pleasure of literature resides in the experience readers have with it, then what would keep our students from having the very kinds of experiences that we value so much with the texts we are suspicious of?

If you Google "the pleasure of reading" you'll find pages and pages of quotes like this one from Malcolm X: "I have often reflected upon the new vistas that reading opened to me. I knew right there in prison that reading had changed forever the course of my life. As I see it today, the ability to read awoke in me some long dormant craving to be mentally alive." If you're a reader, you know what Emily Dickinson meant when she wrote "There is no Frigate like a Book." And yet if you were a student you also know that rather than celebrating the power and pleasure of reading, school can turn it to pure drudgery, a point we heard made again and again in our study of the literate lives of young men (Smith & Wilhelm, 2002; 2006).

If we want to develop engaged and competent readers, might we not benefit from understanding the nature of reading pleasure, particularly in relation to the books that students love, but that we, as adults and teachers, might disapprove of? So we set off to explore young people's reading "where love and need are one." We wanted to understand both its work and play. We wanted to understand the pleasure young people take from what they read, especially their voluntary reading of marginalized texts, what many adults might call "trash." We wanted to consider what might happen if we could unite our goals as teachers with the passions of our students as readers.

Interestingly, on the day we drafted this introduction, March 22, 2013, the *New York Times* ran the article "Straight through the Heart" by Grinnell English professor Dean Bakopoulus. He writes:

Back when I was teaching first-year composition at a large state school, I'd often lament with my colleagues that so many of our incoming students hated to read (we were instructed not to use texts more than a few pages long). We bemoaned the fact that many had left high school without even knowing how to write a sentence.

Bakapoulus continues by maintaining that students need "to think about literature as stories to love, the way many of them did as children."

What they really want is to have some kind of firsthand, visceral relationship with a book. . . . Love, after all, isn't a passive process. Just as a chemistry student doesn't want to lean back and watch an experiment in class, my students don't like to be told to sit around and admire something simply because it is theoretically or historically significant. They want to formulate their own theorem, to write their own code. . . . [W]e do the work because we grow to love the work. After that? Well, with love, all things are possible.

In this book, we will explore the nature of the love students have for, and the pleasures they experience with, the texts they freely choose to read despite a lack of adult approval. We will also explore the benefits they receive from their reading, what reading might make possible for them both now and in the future. We found that these possibilities are indeed profound.

CHAPTER 2

Reading Pleasure

Taking a Closer Look

We're readers. When we tell the stories of our lives, our reading plays a major role. From the third through the seventh grade, Jeff read every Hardy Boys mystery several times, trading books with his friends Bobby Fisher and Bret Bartolovich. He collected all 58 original books. Many years later, when his mother sold the books in a garage sale, he was heartbroken. It was as if she had sold some of his best friends and best experiences. In high school, he became passionate about the novels and poetry of Hermann Hesse. He particularly remembers his first reading of *Steppenwolf*, his love of the character Hermione, and how he used her to think about his own relationships with women. Over the years Jeff has returned to the book many times, with each reading becoming more deep and fulfilling. More recently, just before Jeff's father passed away, Jeff and his dad thoroughly enjoyed a book club discussion of *Plainsong* by Kent Haruf, during which Jeff's father offered some central insights about the genre and topic of plainsongs that helped the group to solve a kind of puzzle—that is, how the book's construction reflected the nature of a plainsong to create certain meanings and effects. When Jeff's wife Peggy was in the deepest throes of a life and death struggle with a vascular disorder and was in a coma for two months, Jeff and his daughter Jasmine bonded over a reading of Alfred Lansing's *Endurance: Shackleton's Incredible Voyage*, perhaps the greatest survival story of all time. They repeated the quote of a historian to each other: "For planning, give me Byrd, for execution: Amundsen. But when the chips are down: *Give me Shackleton!*" When things were especially tough in dealing with Peggy's illness, they would look at each other and say "Give me Shackleton!" often smile, and get back down to business, doing what could be done instead of wallowing in self-pity.

Michael has had similar experiences. When he was in seventh grade, he read John F. Carson's *The Twenty-Third Street Crusaders* perhaps 30 times, glorying in the hours he got to spend with the characters. Just this year he ran into someone else who was a big fan of the book and he was astonished to realize that he still remembered the characters' names 45 years later. He had a bittersweet experience reading Peter J. Rabinowitz's *Before Reading*, thinking all the while that it was going to be amazingly useful in his work and that it was just the kind of book he would have liked to have written had he been smart enough. There was also the time in graduate school when the mysteries of George Herbert's "Artillery" opened up to him. And perhaps most memorably, the summer before his first year in high school when his dad, an inveterate reader himself, gave Michael his copy of *Manchild in the Promised Land,* Claude Brown's memoir of coming of age in Harlem, saying "Here. Read this. It's something you should know about"—an event that triggered Michael's development of a social and political conscience.

The pleasures we've received from reading are among the most memorable we've experienced. But we don't think that we've given pleasure—either the immediate lived-through pleasure of reading or the deep long-lasting psychological satisfactions reading can deliver—the attention it deserves in our writing and thinking about how to teach literature and reading. The purpose of this book is to do just that.

Our journey to writing *Reading Unbound* began many years ago. Jeff has had a free choice reading and literature circle program as part of his classes for over 30 years. Very early on he became fascinated by students—often reluctant readers in school—who would ravenously read books that were marginalized by many teachers and other adults when given the chance. These voracious readers, readers who so obviously took great pleasure in their independent reading, often engaged only superficially, if at all, with the readings that Jeff so loved, readings that he offered to his students as rare and valuable gifts.

While neglecting their homework, even the most reluctant of these students would be reading. Astonishingly, some read 600, 700, even 800 minutes a week. These supposed non-readers would sometimes form friendship groups around their free-choice reading, talking passionately together about authors and trading books and ideas. The more he paid attention, the more Jeff recognized that these students were regularly engaging in the kinds of transactional activities and modes of thought that he was striving for in class (Wilhelm, 2008; Wilhelm & Novak, 2011). But old habits die hard, so he often found himself encouraging these students to try a "better" text; that is, something more in line with what's taught in school. Sometimes students would try one of his suggestions; more often they did not. Eventually he came to understand that his students' engagement with the books they chose themselves was a highly literary transaction (Wilhelm, 2008). His students were reading versions of canonical literature and classic genres. The more he discussed their reading choices with his students, the more he became convinced that these readers were not only reading passionately with great enjoyment, but were also engaging with archetypal themes of great import that would be of great help to them in their life journeys.

These ideas coalesced when students from Noble High School in Maine performed their own drama at the Reading Stephen King conference Jeff helped organize at the University of Maine in the fall of 1998. They did a series of skits on censorship, each ending with the chorus: "But this book could help me!" As you'll soon see, we believe that getting immediate functional help is one kind of pleasure that reading can provide. But Jeff began to think both about what other kinds of pleasure different kinds of books might offer to students and about how he might build bridges from what so engaged his students outside school to what they were doing inside school.

Michael has always been interested in the extent to which Jeff gave his students choice, and the enjoyment this seemed to promote. Although he encouraged his students' out-of-school reading, free-choice reading was never as important a part of his practice as it was for Jeff. In part, his reluctance to make it more central stemmed from his concern over some of the books his students carried with them to class. Sword and sorcery books filled with misogyny; series books like *Sweet Valley High* that seemed to celebrate unrealistic body images that were, in the words of one blogger, "filled with classist/racist/heterosexist rhetoric" (Kareem, 2008). But even then Michael worried that his critiques of his students' reading might be too facile.

Michael also has to admit that another part of his reluctance was that he feared that such books shut him out. "If we read those books in class," he said on more than one occasion, "what would you need me for?" In other words, since Michael didn't know the books—and had nothing to say about them—it seemed as though they undermined his role as instructor. He spent more time thinking about what he could give students in his teaching than what they got from their reading.

Part of our ongoing professional conversation, therefore, has been about why kids read what they read and what that should mean for us as teachers and parents. That's why when Jeff undertook a formal study of the independent readers who have intrigued him for so long, Michael was happy to help him think through the design and delighted when Jeff asked him to help analyze and write up the data. Before we describe the research design and findings, however, we want to share the research and theory that has guided our efforts.

WHAT WE CAN LEARN FROM READING RESEARCH

Much of our previous work has focused on fostering students' active engagement (Wilhelm, 2008)—for example, motivating students to read and write (Smith & Wilhelm, 2002; 2006) and helping them experience the satisfaction of reading and writing well done (Wilhelm, 2007; Smith & Wilhelm, 2010). Additionally, nearly two decades ago, Michael published a study (Smith & Young, 1995) on students' enjoyment of short stories (more on that later). Still, we've never brought the issue of reading pleasure front and center in our professional work. We're not sure why exactly. Maybe it's because we didn't want our readers to think of us as frivolous, especially in an era in which the Common Core State Standards have so clearly focused literacy education on college and career readiness. In our most recent work about the teaching of argumentative, informational, and narrative text structures to meet the CCSS (Smith, Wilhelm, & Fredricksen, 2012; Wilhelm, Smith, & Fredricksen 2012; Fredricksen, Wilhelm, & Smith, 2012), we've argued that we believe the Common Core can be used to trigger and promote progressive practice, explaining, for example, that, "We believe that instruction directed toward improving student performance on standards-based assessments *must* be the most powerful and engaging instruction we can possibly offer" (Smith, Wilhelm, & Fredricksen, 2012, p. 7). But, to the extent that we allude to pleasure through the mention of engagement, it is pleasure in instruction rather than pleasure in reading. And in our arguments we cast that instructional pleasure as important not as an end in itself but because of its instrumental benefits.

We're not alone in an emphasis on instrumentality. In fact, this emphasis seems to be unquestioned in policy discussions. Whenever we talk about reading or learning, there is a focus on specific kinds of results. As one example, the 2004 National Endowment for the Arts created quite a stir with its "bleak assessment of the decline of [literary] reading's role in the nation's culture" (p. vii). Why the gloom?

> *Novels, short stories, poetry, and plays have their own intrinsic value, as do all of the arts. Beyond the benefits of literature to the individual lie the benefits to a culture as a whole. Who reads literary works, what kinds, how often, and how much—all measure the well being of a culture. (p. 1)*

Later the report champions literary reading as the "baseline for participation in social life" which makes it "essential to a sound and healthy understanding of, and participation in democratic society" (p. 1). Nary a mention of pleasure or even the actual experience of reading. The 2009 NEA Report celebrates a reversal of the decline by noting,

"Cultural decline is not inevitable" (p. 2) and by alluding once more to the corollary benefits of literary reading rather than the pleasure one can take from it.

Reading research does a better job taking up the issue of pleasure in its investigations of two related constructs: attitude toward reading and reading motivation. We'll draw on two recent articles to characterize work in these areas. In their examination of the reading attitudes of middle-school students, McKenna and his colleagues (McKenna, Conradi, Lawrence, Jang, & Meyer, 2012) draw on Fishbein and Ajzen (1975) to explain that

> *attitude is acquired, not innate, and is the product of innumerable episodes. Each episode has both a direct effect on attitude and also an indirect effect by shaping the individual's belief structure. These beliefs include predictions about the object (e.g., pleasurable, boring, frustrating) and about how socially significant others view it. To sum up, the three factors affecting attitude acquisition are (1) direct experiences with the object, (2) beliefs about the object, and (3) social norms involving the object . . . concerning the object (contingent on one's propensity to conform to such norms). (p. 284)*

As you can see, their emphasis is not the nature of readers' experience with texts, but rather the extent to which those experiences contribute to a "learned predisposition to respond in a consistently favorable or unfavorable manner with respect to a given object" (Fishbein & Ajzen, p. 6), in this case reading.

McKenna et al. (2012) note that their construct is very much the same as what might be called *reading interest*. But they note further that interest is usually rendered as a plural form and carries the meaning of interest in particular topics and genres. In those terms, our reading interests develop in part because of the pleasure that we have taken in reading, but McKenna and his colleagues do not investigate the nature of that pleasure in their work.

As Schiefele, Schaffner, Möller, and Wigfield (2012) explain, researchers examining reading motivation come closer to addressing pleasure, especially those who seek to understand the dimensions of reading motivation. Much of that work is analyses of survey responses, though some of those surveys used items that were generated from an analysis of interviews or extended written responses. Schiefele and his colleagues found that these quantitative analyses in large measure jibe with those of the few qualitative examinations of reading motivation. They conclude "the following should be regarded as genuine dimensions of reading motivation: curiosity, involvement, competition, recognition, grades, compliance, and work avoidance" (p. 458). But they recognize that qualitative studies "have suggested that the experience of reading involves several distinguishable facets (e.g., absorption, enjoyment, relaxation) that may warrant further analysis" (p. 457). These facets in need of further analysis would seem to be closer to what we think of when we talk about the experience of pleasure one may take from reading.

In a report published by the National Literacy Trust in the United Kingdom, Clark and Rumbold (2006) take a different tack both from McKenna et al.'s (2012) research and from the research reviewed by Schiefele and his colleagues (2012). In their view, reading for pleasure "refers to reading that we to do of our own free will anticipating the satisfaction that we will get from the act of reading. It also refers to reading that having begun at someone else's request we continue because we are interested in it" (p. 5). However, their justification for their focus on pleasure is, once again, instrumental. That is, reading pleasure is important because of "its impact on literacy attainment and other outcomes" (p. 5) rather than because of the experience it provides. More specifically, they argue that research has established that reading for pleasure is positively associated with reading achievement, writing ability, comprehension, vocabulary development, positive attitudes about reading, self-confidence in reading, and pleasure reading in later life.

Just as this book was going to press (September, 2013), a sophisticated new study from the UK appeared that makes an even more dramatic claim. We thought the study was important enough that we stopped the presses so we could discuss it here. "Social Inequalities in Cognitive Scores at Age 16: The Role of Reading" (Sullivan & Brown) draws on data collected in the 1970 British Cohort Study which is following the lives of more than 17,000 people born in England, Scotland, and Wales in a single week of 1970. Researchers in that longitudinal study have collected follow-up data from the study's participants at ages 5, 10, 16, 26, 30, 34, 38, and 42. Sullivan and Brown drew on these data to investigate "whether inequalities due to social background are similar across the three domains of vocabulary, spelling, and mathematics, or whether they differ and to what extent these inequalities are accounted for by family material and cultural resources" (p. 2). After doing a series of multiple analyses, they conclude the following:

> Our findings . . . [suggest] that children's leisure reading is important for educational attainment and social mobility . . . and suggest that the mechanism for this is increased cognitive development. Once we controlled for the child's test scores at age five and ten, the influence of the child's own reading remained highly significant, suggesting that the positive link between leisure reading and cognitive outcomes is not purely due to more able children being more likely to read a lot, but that reading is actually linked to increased cognitive progress over time. From a policy perspective, this strongly supports the need to support and encourage children's reading in their leisure time. (p. 37)

The increased cognitive processes are what account for the surprising finding that leisure reading actually was correlated with math performance.

Taken together, the studies that examine the impact of leisure reading make a compelling case for its importance. We want to stress that we believe that such work is crucially important, so when we note that discussions of the pleasure of reading take an instrumental view, we're not offering a critique. However, if educators are to pursue a policy of supporting and encouraging the pleasure reading of young people, we have to have a deeper understanding of its nature and varieties than the instrumental studies provide.

One theorist who focuses on the nature of pleasurable reading experiences is Roland Barthes (1975). Barthes makes a distinction between pleasure and bliss, though he is wary of "absolute classifications" (p. 4). The text of *pleasure,* he says, "contents, fills, grants euphoria: the text that comes from a culture and does not break with it, is linked to a *comfortable* practice of reading" (p. 14). (Interestingly, he uses the same notion of comfort that Radway does in "Reading Is Not Eating" [1986].) The text of *bliss,* on the other hand,

> imposes a state of loss . . ., unsettles the reader's historical, cultural, psychological assumptions, the consistency of his tastes, values, memories, brings to a crisis his relation with language. (p. 14)

According to Barthes, conventional or familiar texts yield a pleasure that is safe and comfortable, a kind of pleasure he doesn't much admire, while experimental or unfamiliar ones produce a bliss that is challenging and unsettling. Bliss is produced by the kinds of reading experiences recommended by Kafka in a letter to Oskar Pollack, "that bite and sting us" and that "smash the frozen seas within."

Barthes' ideas are difficult to write about because they are so abstract and metaphoric, but he plays with three ideas that have affected our thinking. First, although we question the hierarchy that Barthes suggests, we're persuaded by his argument that textual pleasure isn't singular. That means to understand pleasure, one needs to delineate its forms, something we attempt to do in the coding of our data. Second, textual pleasure is something that's experienced by individual readers:

> Pleasure, however, is not an element of the text, it is not a naïve residue; it does not depend on a logic of understanding and on sensation; it is a drift, something both revolutionary and asocial. And it cannot be taken over by any collectivity, any mentality, any idiolect." (p. 23)

We agree, which is why we interviewed individual readers.

Third, textual pleasure is not distinct from the other pleasures of our lives. As he explains, "There is supposed to be a mystique of the Text. On the contrary, the whole effort consists in materializing the pleasure of the text, in making the text an object of pleasure like the others" (p. 58). And later: "The important thing is to equalize the field of pleasure, to abolish the false opposition of practical life and contemplative life" (p. 59). This recognition is why we turned to philosophers in addition to literary theorists and reading researchers to help us understand our data.

In short, although research on reading interests abounds, as Clark and Rumbold (2006) note, the investigation of "reading for pleasure has not been a research priority" (p. 9). The research that does exist tends to be focused on the benefits of reading for pleasure and the extent to which people do, in fact, read. But think for a minute about how we so often say that we want to encourage students to become lifelong readers. They aren't going to be if they don't take pleasure in the act. If we're going to foster their pleasure, we have to understand it. Understanding the pleasures of reading may not have been a research priority. But it should be.

Victor Nell's (1988) *Lost in a Book: The Psychology of Reading for Pleasure* is an exception to the rule. Nell's work is most like our own in that its primary goal is to understand the nature of reading pleasure. On the basis of a variety of studies, Nell built a model of what he calls "ludic reading"—a state of blissful engagement avid readers enter when consuming books for pleasure. He argues that reading for pleasure is unlikely to occur, or even be attempted, unless the necessary antecedents are in place: reading ability, a positive attitude to reading (in the sense that McKenna and his colleagues [2012] describe it) and the appropriate book, both in terms of its match to the reader's ability and its match to the reader's interest. If those antecedents are in place, a reader will choose to begin reading. Once a reader has begun reading, he or she pays a kind of effortless attention to the text (the continuing impulse to read), employing both automated reading skills and consciously controlled comprehension processes. The result, says Nell are both physiological and cognitive changes that he describes very poetically:

These are the paired wonders of reading: the world creating power of books, and the reader's effortless absorption that allows the book's fragile world, all air and thought, to maintain itself for a while, a bamboo and paper house among earthquakes; within it readers acquire peace, become more powerful, feel braver and wiser in ways of the world." (p. 1)

We've condensed Nell's 300 pages into just a paragraph, but that paragraph raises the question of what we can add to Nell's findings. Two things, we think. First, the youngest of Nell's participants were college students; ours are adolescents. Readers of different ages may experience pleasure differently. Second, Nell seems to equate the trance-like state one may enter while reading a narrative with pleasure. The stories with which we began this chapter about our own reading, Barthes's distinction between pleasure and bliss, and the data we will soon be sharing suggest that rather than seeking to describe the pleasure of reading, we should be investigating its varieties.

In earlier related work, Michael tried to address these concerns (Smith & Young, 1995). On the basis of a self-study and an analysis of 169 seventh through twelfth graders' written explanations of why they liked their favorite book or story, he wrote a survey to operationalize three different dimensions of what he was calling "liking" of a story. The items themselves are in parentheses:

- liking the surface features of a story (*I like this type of story. I like stories by this author. This story was easy to read. This story is about something interesting. This story is about something important. I like the way the author tells this story. The story is well written. I like stories with these kinds of characters.*)

- liking the experience of reading a story (*This story kept me interested as I was reading it. I really wanted to know what would happen next. This story was a challenge to read. This story made me feel strong emotions as I was reading it. As I was reading this story, I felt as though I was part of its world. This story took me away from my world while I was reading. I like the way this story made me feel as I was reading it. I enjoyed getting to know the characters as I was reading this story. As I read this story, I could picture what was going on. As I was reading this story, I could really relate to the characters.*)

- liking the effects of a story (*This story gave me something to think about. I learned something interesting from this story. I learned something important from this story. Reading this story made me respect the author. This story made me like reading better than I did before. The emotions I felt while I read this story will stay with me long after I finished reading it. This story will affect the way I live my life. Now that I've read this story, I would like to share it with a friend.*)

Michael administered the survey to 118 other adolescents after they had read one of four stories that they were randomly assigned, asking them to mark strongly agree, agree, disagree, or strongly disagree for each survey item. An analysis of students' responses to the survey revealed that, as he had expected, students' liking of a story begins with their liking the surface features of the story, proceeds to their liking of their experience while reading the story, and continues to their liking of the effect the story had on them.

That is, adolescents gravitate to texts whose surface features match an existing interest. Once they pick up those texts, they value the quality of the experience that they have while reading. The texts that they like the most are ones that stay with them in some way once the reading is over. However, like Nell, Michael focused only on reading a particular kind of narrative. His survey wouldn't be as useful in assessing a student's liking of the myriad other kinds of texts that exist.

Searching for Answers in Philosophy

Previous reading research didn't speak as directly to the pleasure of reading as we had hoped, so we turned to philosophy to help us think about the issue. Fred Feldman's (2004) *Pleasure and the Good Life: Concerning the Nature, Varieties, and Plausibility of Hedonism* has been especially useful. Feldman's project is "to defend hedonism as a substantive theory about the Good Life," by which he means "the life that is good in itself for the one who lives it" (p. 1) as opposed to, say, society at large. Feldman offers a defense of what he calls Intrinsic Attitudinal Hedonism. In brief, he argues that the value of a life to one who lives it is the measure of the intrinsic attitudinal pleasure he or she experiences minus the intrinsic pain he or she experiences. It seems simple, but, of course, it's not. Feldman has to address numerous questions about, and objections to, his formulation; for example, how he can compare the relative merit of pleasures of the body and pleasures of the mind, and how his argument might address someone's taking pleasure in something evil, disgusting, or hurtful to others. Because our focus is on reading, many of those objections aren't germane. But we found his formulation very compelling, so let's take a look at its elements.

According to Feldman, the amount of attitudinal pleasure that someone takes is determined by the pleasure's intensity and duration. He notes also that there is a "plurality of pleasure" and that a person can enjoy "multiple, temporally overlapping pleasures" (p. 60). He explains that temporality further, noting that one can take pleasure in "facts about the past, present, or future" (p. 61).

Feldman does not provide a taxonomy of types of pleasures, so we turned elsewhere for help thinking about that variety. As is so often the case, we found that the work of John Dewey was most fruitful, specifically his *Interest and Effort in Education* (1913). Although we noted a distinction between interest and pleasure in reading research, Dewey takes pains to unite them right from the start of his book. The genuine principle of interest, he says,

> is the principle of the recognized identity of the fact to be learned or the
> action proposed with the growing self; that it lies in the direction of the
> agent's own growth, and is, therefore, imperiously demanded, if the agent is
> to be himself. (p. 7)

Dewey explicitly links the identity of the activity and the evolving identity of the individual with pleasure. The type of pleasure Dewey endorses is the pleasure found in

the accompaniment of activity. It is found wherever there is successful achievement, mastery, getting on. It is the personal phase of an outgoing energy. This sort of pleasure is always absorbed in the activity itself. It has no separate existence. This is the type of pleasure found in legitimate interest. (p. 12)

Legitimate interest is related to outgrowing oneself in some way and this outgrowing gives rise to pleasure. And, according to Dewey, this pleasure can take different forms. One is what Dewey calls *play*. The essential characteristic of play is that it is a sensory experience, a kind of experience that harkens back to the physiological changes that Nell explains are linked to readers' abandoning themselves to the world of a story. According to Dewey, people engage in play for the experience itself, not for some other reason. Here's how he puts it:

There are cases where action is direct and immediate. It puts itself forth with no thought of anything beyond. It satisfies in and of itself. The end is the present activity, and so there is no gap in the mind between means and end. All play is of this immediate character. (p. 21)

In our view, then, pleasure in play is found in readers' giving themselves over completely to the story world and the experience of that world, as Jeff did when he was reading *The Hardy Boys* and as Michael did when he reread *The Twenty-Third Street Crusaders* in order to spend more time with the characters.

Play is distinct from another kind of pleasure, the pleasure of work. Dewey explains that in both play and work the child focuses on the immediate experience:

A child engaged in making something with tools, say, a boat, may be just as immediately interested in what he is doing as if he were sailing the boat. He is not doing what he does for the mere sake of an external result—the boat—nor for the mere sake of sailing it later. The thought of the finished product and of the use to which it is to be put may come to his mind, but so as to enhance his immediate activity of construction. (p. 79)

What distinguishes work from play is the mediation of tools, either physical or cognitive:

Work in the sense in which it has been defined covers all activities involving the use of intervening materials, appliances, and forms of skill consciously used in achieving results. It covers all forms of expression and construction with tools and materials, all forms of artistic and manual activity so far as they involve the conscious or thoughtful endeavor to achieve an end. (pp. 80-81)

Readers who use texts as tools experience the pleasure of work. We want to stress, though, that the nature of that work varies widely. Our stories in the introduction give a sense of that variety. The work that Jeff described was intensely personal. When he first read Hesse's *Steppenwolf* while in high school, he read and re-read the scenes with Hermione, totally intrigued with her and her relationship to Hermann. He felt that he knew Hermione. Not until he reread the book as an adult did he understand how Hermione represented the *anima* of Hermann—his repressed feminine side—his as-yet unrealized capacities for caring and nurturance—and that he recognized her figure from his own dreams, calling him to deeper relationships with family and friends. This example illustrates an insight from depth psychology, which maintains that there is no way to the deep meanings of life except through symbol and story. One kind of work that reading does is to plumb those deep meanings. Another kind of work is more quotidian as when Michael was reading *Before Reading*, taking pleasure all the while in knowing how it would be useful in his subsequent teaching and writing.

These pleasures reside not so much in figuring things out but in recognizing that the reading we were doing could be part of a "thoughtful endeavor to achieve an end." As Dewey (1913) puts it, in such cases the intellectual interest [is] subordinate . . . to the accomplishment of a process." He continues:

But it is also possible for it to become a dominating interest, so that instead of thinking things out and discovering them for the sake of the successful achievement of an activity, we institute the activity for the sake of finding out something. Then the distinctively intellectual, or theoretical, interest shows itself. (p. 82)

The pleasure we take in figuring things out, the kind of pleasure Jeff experienced when discussing *Plainsong* with his father and book club, figuring out during the discussion how the book itself reflected the construction of a plainsong and the meanings expressed by this kind of text, and Michael experienced when he thought he finally understood "Artillery" are what, following Dewey, we are calling "intellectual pleasures."

Finally, Dewey notes that children are profoundly social, a contention that resonates with one of our chief findings in our study (Smith & Wilhelm, 2002) of literate lives of young men both in and out of school. It is practically impossible, Dewey writes, to realize

*the extent to which children are concerned with things only as they enter into
and affect the concerns of persons, and the extent to which a personal-social
interest radiates upon objects and gives them their meaning and worth. (p. 86)*

Social pleasure, then, is engaging with and learning about others. We believe
something more is involved, though, something Dewey didn't talk about because he
focused on young children who, he says, identify their own concerns with those of
others. In adolescence, one's job is not just to identify with others as a way to develop a
moral sense, but also to differentiate oneself from others. Social pleasure, then, is of two
sorts: a learning about others but also a kind of identity work, that is, a distinguishing of
oneself from others.

You can see those dimensions illustrated in our introductory paragraphs. Michael's
reading of *Manchild in the Promised Land* was enormously important (and pleasurable) to
him because he learned so much about a life that was so different from his own. Jeff's
reading of *Endurance* was so important (and pleasurable) to him because it bonded him
with his daughter at a time of great stress. He was also able to see himself as the kind
of reader who could make connections between his reading and his life in ways that
inspired and helped him through challenges.

Our Study

We undertook this study because we wanted to find out more about how these notions
of pleasure in reading played out with adolescents. The study we report in these pages
is divided into two parts. In Part 1 we explore the nature and variety of the pleasures
committed readers of genres that are typically not taught or approved of in school
take from their reading. We identified these genres (romance, vampire stories, horror,
dystopian fiction, and fantasy) by thinking about our own teaching and through
informal conversations with other teachers. We solicited our student readers through a
survey of reading behaviors administered to all of the eighth graders in a school with
which Jeff has a long-standing relationship. Fourteen students identified themselves as
committed readers of these genres and agreed to participate in the study. (Our promises
of anonymity keep us from revealing any additional information about them.) Jeff
conducted multiple one-on-one interviews with the participants, asking them to explain
what they had been reading and how they felt about it. During these interviews he asked
them to bring in a favorite book and to "think aloud" while they were reading. He also
asked them to compare their reading to their other literate activities, focusing especially
on gaming as all of our committed readers were committed gamers as well.

We transcribed these interviews and parsed them into content units, that is, a segment of discourse designed to make a single point. These units varied in length from a clause to several exchanges in dialogue. For example, in this excerpt from Callie's first interview, "Reading for me is mostly about enjoyment, and I know in school it can kind of get twisted out of enjoyment cuz there are some books I'd rather not read in school," the first clause was determined to be one unit because it makes a point about her primary reason for reading and the next two clauses became a second unit that makes a point about reading in school. In the next example from Paul, the unit is much longer because throughout his conversational turn he is making a single point about the benefits of pliable texts:

> [The] special appeal of fantasy is the pliable text, that you can play with the text and you can see the text and you can feel the text and you can hear the text, you can build onto the text and kind of, 'cause a good fantasy writer to me will make his text so you can reread it in a completely different way and see it through different eyes.

We coded the content units using the qualitative software program atlas.ti. Based on the review of relevant research and theory we shared above, we started with three of what atlas.ti calls *coding families*: the nature of pleasure; the conditions that give rise to it; and related constructs, such as attitude toward reading, reading interests, and motivation to read. When we coded for the nature of pleasure, we coded for the four dimensions of pleasure we discussed previously (type, intensity, duration, timing). We used Dewey's (1913) four kinds of educative interest in our initial coding of the type of pleasure and then went back and reread the data to identify subthemes in each type. Sometimes the type of pleasure was clear—as when Karen says, "Well you can definitely feel like you're the character so you are kind of living through it and what would it be like to live like that." This content unit unambiguously describes the pleasure of play, focusing as it does on the immediate pleasure of entering a story world. However, the four types of interest sometimes overlapped as in the following comment from Robert:

> I do want it to be entertaining at the same time cuz I'm reading *Siddhartha* by Herman Hesse, and the thing that I like about that book is he does provide you the beautiful imagery but it doesn't go so deeply that you're just, "Can you get to the point now?" He provides [the point] in way that wraps around the story also, so that you want to keep reading.

Robert seems to us to be commenting both on the playful pleasure of entering a story world and also the intellectual pleasure of understanding a theme. In such cases we made a judgment about which pleasure was more salient. In this case we think his emphasis is on imagery and story, so we coded his comment as a play pleasure. If we were uncertain of our judgment, we gave the content unit two codes for type of pleasure. Throughout the book we'll be presenting lots of our data, so you'll be able to assess whether you agree with the coding that we did. Figure 1 presents our coding scheme in outline form.

Those of you who know Feldman's work will recognize that our coding does not take up a fifth dimension of pleasure that Feldman (2004) discusses: altitude. Although he argues that "every episode of attitudinal pleasure is intrinsically good" (p. 75), he also argues that objects of pleasure "can be ranked on a scale according to its suitability to serve as an object of such pleasure" (p. 73-74). The altitude of a pleasure, according to Feldman, is a measure of its worthiness. But, as we discussed last chapter, determining the worthiness of a text is at best a problematic enterprise. Radway's (1984) foundational research has taught us that readers use books that other people call "trash" in surprising ways. We've learned from Nell (1988) that the ludic readers he studied regarded nearly half of their reading as "trash," conditioned, no doubt, by the centuries' worth of condemnation of mass reading that Nell chronicles. And most importantly, as you'll soon see, we learned from the young people with whom we worked about the pleasures they took from texts that others might dismiss.

In Part 2 of the study Jeff interviewed a new set of informants, dedicated high school and first-year college readers of those same genres. We supplemented these data with entries from Jeff's teaching journal. Over the years, he had gathered observations, surveys, and assessments—as well as notes on informal conversations he had with interest/friendship groups organized around the same genres in our study. We did a case study of each of the five genres, relating each case to the analysis we did in Part 1, focusing especially on how the elements of pleasure can be illuminated by depth psychology.

Pleasure, says social psychologist Nico Frijda (2001), has great "motivating power. It pushes and clamors for continuation, it instigates desire, it is at the root of human passion" (p. 72). If we want to harness that motivating power, we have to understand it. So let's get started, beginning with the pleasure of play.

Figure 1

Coding Scheme

Nature of Pleasure Code Family

- Types of Pleasure
  - ✓ Play pleasure
  - ✓ Work pleasure
  - ✓ Intellectual pleasure
  - ✓ Social pleasure
- Intensity of pleasure
- Duration of pleasure
- Timing of pleasure
  - ✓ Before reading
  - ✓ During reading
  - ✓ After reading

Conditions for Pleasure Code Family

- Text
  - ✓ Genre
  - ✓ Topic
  - ✓ Length
  - ✓ Style
- Gaming

Related Constructs

- Attitude towards reading
- Attitude towards school
- Attitude towards school reading

CHAPTER 3

PLAY PLEASURE

"I Just Get This Joy Reading"

Michael's granddaughter Gabrielle lives with him and his wife Karen. Michael has the more flexible schedule, so he's on drop-off and pick-up duty. Sometimes he doesn't take Gabby home right away from aftercare and instead takes her for a quick dinner and then on errands. Whenever that happens, Gabby begins negotiating immediately: "There'll be time for play, right, Pop-Pop? We can still play, right?" There's no chance to get her cooperation without an answer in the affirmative. Play, you see, is precious to Gabby. Without an abacus, you probably can't count the games crammed into the entertainment center in Michael's family room. Gabby's not the only one for whom play is precious.

Walk into Jeff's garage and you'll be astonished at all his gear for outdoor play: kayaks and bikes and tents and helmets and skis. Not to be outdone, Jeff's wife Peggy is an aficionado of card and board games. Don't think you can visit the Wilhelms and get away without a game of cribbage or *Settlers of Catan*.

Research, such as the seminal work of D. W. Winnicott (1971), tells us that play is an integral tool for learning and human development. Winnicott famously wrote that "On the basis of playing is built the whole of [humanity]'s experiential existence" (p. 64). It is through imagination games and role-play that children learn to take risks. Risk-taking is crucial to every kind of learning since one is trying to do what one cannot yet do.

In *Play: How It Shapes the Brain, Opens the Imagination, and Invigorates the Soul* (2009), Stuart Brown documents neurological and ethological research that shows how play is the central complex of evolved behaviors developed to facilitate learning and social bonding among mammals. Social imagination is facilitated through members' sportive, artful, innovative participation within loosely rule-governed guidelines. There is actual evolutionary truth to the saying "All work and no play makes Jack a dull boy."

Why? Dewey points out that play is the primary mechanism by which young children learn. Vygotsky (1978) agrees. He famously proclaims that "in play, it is as though a child were always a head taller than himself" (p. 102). In other words, in play we are always outgrowing our current selves. Think of small children's role-playing. They never role-play being less intelligent or less powerful or less competent than they are but instead always role-play being smarter and more competent. In this way, play is the harbinger of growth and capacity yet to come. Adults experience this benefit of play as well. For example, if your principal makes you angry, don't tell us that you don't do a little role-play in your mind—a role-play in which you are more informed, capable, and powerful than you might be in real life. Such role-playing, either external or internal, can be immensely pleasurable and satisfying (Wilhelm, 2012b; Wilhelm & Edmiston, 1998).

The readers in our study likewise valued play and demonstrated the extent to which reading is a form of play. You might recall from the last chapter that play, according to Dewey, is a sensory experience in which one engages for the purpose of the experience itself. In that way, it's reminiscent of the flow experiences we discussed in our study of the literate lives of young men (Smith & Wilhelm, 2002; 2006), especially the quality we refer to as a focus on the immediate.

It might seem odd to talk about reading in terms of sensory pleasure, but as we'll see, our participants did so. Frijda helps explain why. He argues that "many pleasures of the senses are not fully accounted for by their sensory nature. They are pleasures that depend on overall states of the organism or on being immersed in emotions of different sorts" (p. 79). Let's take a look at some of those emotions and consider the extent to which they are a function of the kind of sensory experiences that characterize play.

Experiencing the Pleasure of Play in General Terms

We coded nearly 500 of the 1400 content units in the interviews as relating to play pleasure. In some of those units, our participants talked in general terms about the pleasure of reading. Here's Paul in a quote that so resonates with us that it informed our chapter subtitle: "And I read because I love it, I just get this joy reading. . . . It doesn't have any restrictions to it." That is, a book provides an arena in which Paul can stand a head taller than himself, an arena in which others can't place limits on what he does. John echoed Paul's remark: "I basically read . . . for entertainment. I just read for fun." Both young men emphasize the experience of reading rather than anything they take from it. Helen made that emphasis explicit: "I don't pick up a book to learn things. I pick up a book to have fun reading it."

So did Callie. She offered a telling contrast between what she read for herself and what she read for school:

> I think school reading can also be about things you'll want to know or you'll need to know, but when you're reading a book at home you're learning stuff that you want to know, but you're also enjoying it when you do it. When you're reading a book for school, sometimes that enjoyment can be lost, and it can just be about learning, but home reading is a lot more fun.

She made a similar point in talking about Chuck Palahniuk's *Invisible Monsters*:

> It was about a supermodel and it turns out like her brother, she thought he had died but he had become a drag queen but after her accident she met him in the hospital and they became really close but he didn't know she was his sister and so they related in that way and then it turns out in the end that she was the reason, she purposely caused the accident that disfigured her. It was a really weird, interesting book, but like I was just reading it. I was reading it based purely on the plot line, and I wasn't really thinking about how it could relate to my life. And then when I was put into a situation where I was thinking about my life the book came up.

Learning occurs in home reading, Callie tells us, but that's not what it's for. In fact, it seems that learning from home reading is almost accidental—just as the learning from play is typically an accidental by-product. What's important is the fun. In school the necessity of learning trumps pleasure, and, it seems, often dissipates that fun.

The Pleasure of Entering a Story World

Our participants were wonderfully articulate about the pleasure of leaving their world and entering a story world. Rebecca said she reads "to dissipate the real world. Go somewhere new. Get rid of me and become someone else."

Helen echoed that sentiment:

> I feel like I just read to get the story out of the book and stuff, and it's good to be alone with whatever they're saying in the book, in your own head just thinking about what's happening, and it's like getting away from your own world into somebody else's that could be way cooler, or not so cool.

Karen primarily read fantasy because it worked to provide that get-away:

> Well, for personal preferences I like to choose books because they're interesting and I like to get away kind of when I read, and like find a different world. Like I choose a lot of fantasy because it sparks your imagination and lets you go somewhere else. That's the reason I like to read.

Interestingly, although many teachers see gaming as the mortal enemy of reading, the pleasure of play in gaming very much resembles the pleasure of play in reading. Terry made the comparison explicit:

> I think it [gaming] is kind of like reading because you're in a story, and, I mean, you're not reading letters on a page but you're in a story and that's what reading is: telling a story. Like the best books, I've noticed, are the really engaging ones that are edge of your seat, really engaged books that you can pick up again and again, and that's what I can do with this game. That's why it's my favorite.

Strategies for Entering a Story World

The parts our participants played in the new worlds they get away to were interestingly varied. Karen experiences a book as though she's the main character: "Well you can definitely feel like you're the character so you are kind of living through it and what would it be like to live like that." Helen also talked about how she actually experiences a story world when she reads:

> I get bored with my life sometimes. Not like super bored, like midlife crisis bored, but just reality gets boring sometimes and it's cool to think about other stuff. I'm reading *The Clan of the Cave Bear*, the second one, and it's cool cuz it's not everyday life, it's something I haven't experienced, but I'm sort of semi-experiencing it.

Later in the in interview she picked up this idea once again in an exchange with Jeff:

HELEN: *And sometimes I wish I really was like the characters. For the longest time I wished I was someone who lived in one of the [YA fantasy author] Tamora Pierce's Alanna books. Like, "I must be her! She's soooo cool!" and then later I got over it. I realized, you know, it wouldn't be that great.*

JEFF: *That's an interesting idea. To think about being like the characters. When you say that, do you mean you want to live through what the characters live through, or do you want to have their qualities?*

HELEN: *Live through what they live through AND have their qualities. Like, to be the character in the book and have all of that happen to you. Sometimes it's just really cool to think about that. Like, if I was them and did exactly what they did, that would be so cool.*

And later:

I also like the high intense action battle scenes, because I know for sure I'm never going to be hacking at someone with a broadsword. Might as well experience it via text without actually having to kill someone. Fantasy, like I said before, it's imagination food. That's really the gist of fantasy.

But if Helen can't experience this kind of playful pleasure, she doesn't enjoy reading, which is why she prefers fantasy to historical fiction: "That's the problem with reading historical fiction for me is I always wish I was there. But I don't know what I would do, you know?"

Robert, it seems, entered the story world differently, placing himself in that world instead of inhabiting it as though he were a character:

When I read at home I usually kind of try and find books that I—it kind of lets me think as though I was in the book. I kind of like to be able to enter that world and see what new possibilities would be in it.

So did Mia, as she explained in talking about a favorite manga text:

MIA: *Here's a picture of the manager, and I can see the man so it feels like the outside.*

JEFF:	*So you're in the story?*
MIA:	*Yeah. it kinda feels like I'm in the story.*
JEFF:	*Are there particular things in the picture or in the story that make you feel like you're in it?*
MIA:	*Yeah, like, they look at you.*
JEFF:	*Do they kind of address you or talk to you?*
MIA:	*No.*
JEFF:	*They just kind of look at you.*
MIA:	*Yeah, they kind of make eye contact with you.*

Mia so fully gives herself over to the world of the story that she can feel the characters' glances.

Rebecca, another Tamora Pierce fan, was notable for talking about the variety of approaches she employed for entering a story world:

> The main character in this book is a guy. So I can kind of go into him and be the participant, but it's more if I'm like right next to him kind of thing. So I'm the participant but I'm not really the participant. And at the same time, since I'm reading the book and I'm not in the book, I'm the fly on the wall. So I'm seeing it happen. Now with most of the books I read, the main character is actually a girl. I think that's probably because I'm a girl. My favorite authors, most of the time the main character's a girl. . . . And with that, with the guys I'm next to them but with the girls I'm usually like, "Wow I'm a lot like that sometimes." I connect to how they feel.

Pretty complicated stuff. If the main character is a boy, she acts both as an observer and a quasi-participant. If the main character's a girl, she experiences the story as the character. But that character can change. Look at what she said about Pierce's Alanna series:

REBECCA:	*So I was Alanna while she was becoming a knight. Then I was Diane who is learning to become a wild mage. She meets Alanna all the time. They're friends.*
JEFF:	*So who are you now?*
REBECCA:	*Okay, well, right now in the series, right now I am Ali who is Alanna's daughter and I'm in the fourth series.*

JEFF: *So you're both the daughter and the mom in some ways.*

REBECCA: *Yes. I was the mom and now I'm the daughter. But in the third series there's also Kel. Kel wanted to become a knight, but here is the problem: There are no female knights except Alanna. So now we have to go through becoming a knight again, but actually this time she's actually a girl. Because Alanna became a knight by pretending she was a guy. So now we get to go through it being an actual girl.*

She chooses to become Kel because doing so will allow her to experience becoming a knight in a different way.

But she doesn't always experience things from the perspectives of one of the novel's main characters as the exchange below reveals:

REBECCA: *The evil people are awesome! They can do whatever they want! They can act like complete and utter idiots and they're still evil and so they're cool.*

JEFF: *So why do you like that?*

REBECCA: *Well, well, it's kind of, they can be who they want to be, they can do whatever the heck they want to and be who they want to be. And I like doing that, but I'm not going to go around slaughtering everybody I can see just for the heck of it.*

These playful experiences have a very serious dimension. Our informants talked about the play-based pleasure of overcoming the constraints of one's life and doing things through imagination that one could not, and would not, want to do in real life.

Interestingly, once again, our participants' discussion of how they entered a story world in games very much resembled their discussion of their reading. Rebecca made that connection explicit: "Like I told you before, I like playing games and I like reading books because I become the characters and I go in to the world and stuff."

So did Terry:

I really like FPS games, that's First Person Shooters. Those are really engaging because instead of like a third person where you see the actual person, so you don't feel as connected to the character as you do in a first person because you see the arms when you're playing. If you're an

> experienced gamer you know the controls like a book. You can do anything in those games. If you know that, then you don't really pay attention to what your fingers are doing. A lot of times I'll be playing and I won't even see my hands. They'll be under a blanket or something, because my basement's cold. I'll be under a blanket and I'll feel really connected to a character because it's a first person, so I can try and insert my body to be thinking that what the screen is showing is what my eyes are seeing. So it's really interactive.

Karen's comment about evil characters in games echoes Rebecca's discussion about why she likes evil characters in her reading: "I don't know. It's not really the violence for me. I think it's just the chance to be evil without real consequences." Both girls' comments reflect the liminality of stories. Liminality (from the Latin *limen*) designates a threshold, a psychological or metaphysical state in which one is on the threshold of or between two existential planes. Because the worlds of books and games are both real and unreal at the same time, they provide unique opportunities for experience that we hope our students will never seek in their lives.

Leave it to Rebecca to present another complex way of seeing herself in a gaming world. Here she was talking about *The Sims*:

> Because I'm God! It's fun to have all the power and do whatever I want to do. And so, with Sims, you create and you control this character, so it's kind of you but you're God actually. So you're like their higher self.

Wesley didn't talk about becoming God through his gaming but he did talk about becoming more than he is:

> Back to like the *Assassin's Creed* game, they made it so you can climb up walls using certain things to pull yourself up and I just really love that, because it's like no restrictions. You can't jump high enough, or you can't climb up this or that. You can do what you normally can't do. I can't normally pull myself up a wall, I'm not strong enough. I don't know how. It's just a great way to entertain myself.

As we argued above, the exercise of power and autonomy is essential to play. No child plays being less powerful or less competent than they are in real life. In play, we practice being more than we are. In safe ways, we can test the waters.

The Importance of Sensory Experience

In order to make a move from the world of their lives to the world of the story, our participants drew on sensory experience. Paul made that clear:

> The special appeal of fantasy is the pliable text, that you can play with the text and you can see the text and you can feel the text and you can hear the text, you can build onto the text.

You can see just how rich our participants' sensory experiences were by looking at their think-alouds. Here's Callie reading ee cummings's "All in green went my love riding":

> "All in green went my love riding/on a great horse of gold/into the silver dawn." And I think of that and what beautiful imagery that is. I see this girl, in a green velvet waistcoat on a horse, into the dawn, and how it relates to the colors and the imagery because in each line there is a color and each line has imagery. There's the great horse of gold, which is a metaphor for dawn. "Four lean hounds crouched low and smiling/the merry deer ran before." And I think of like, the fox hunts and the deer hunts with the dogs and the hounds crouching low. The hounds look very menacing and they almost look like people because they're crouching so low, but they have these giant grins like Cheshire cats but with really sharp teeth.

And here's Alex reading David Clement-Davies' *The Sight*:

> "Light began to come. As it grew, Larka shivered, for there was no heat in it. It seemed to make the woods even more fearful, and the air took on a yellowy pallor while the objects that it lit seemed drained of color, grey and lifeless." So again you can kind of see the trees and everything, but instead of seeing them as green and brown and all that, you just see the silhouettes almost of the trees and then that kind of glow of sunlight, but that feeling of being in the middle of winter.

As you can see, the participants in our study were amazingly adept visualizers. Nell (1988) argues that readers have to have the requisite reading ability before ludic reading can take place. Quite clearly, being able to conjure sensory experience from written words is one aspect of that ability. This is something Jeff found as well, particularly in regards to visualization in his studies that led to *You Gotta BE the Book* (2008) and his follow-up intervention work (2012c).

Conjuring sensory experience is so important to entering a story that Rebecca had difficulty doing so if her conjuring was pre-empted by the author:

> With manga they have pictures, too, so you can't really become part of the book. Eventually I'm like a fly on the wall. Especially if I start reading a book and I just like turn the page and that's the only thing that is reality, because I'm just a fly on the wall.

She can't enter as the character as she often likes to do because, in effect, she's been drawn out of the story.

Not all of our readers shared her view, however. Here's Paul talking with Jeff about how the images draw him in when reading Max Allan Collins's *The Road to Perdition*:

PAUL: *Well, with traditional texts like paper and ink and stuff you get like 2D look at things. When you get a 3D text you can see how the author was seeing it and I like that a lot because I can understand this text; it's just that the pictures bring it alive. And I liked how* Road to Perdition *did that. It just had very nice graphics and it was a really well done book, graphic novel.*

JEFF: *What about the graphics did you really like?*

PAUL: *I liked how they popped off the paper. The artist who did it had a very nice style that was almost as if he was just drawing straight lines and then gapping it so that there would be the picture between those lines and it was really cool style that made it pop straight off the paper and made you see it. And also he did a very good job shadowing with that line style.*

We'll be talking about aesthetic pleasure as one kind of intellectual pleasure. But for now, what's important is to note that our participants wanted to, in Paul's words, "bring the story alive."

Of course, in games, the responsibility for the sensory experience resides with the game's creator. But, as Robert explained, involving oneself in creating a sensory experience is nonetheless important:

> This new game [*L.A. Noire*] is really focusing on making their expressions look like they're talking. Their mouths, everything is just them talking. They're putting that to good use because it's a detective story, so like when you are interrogating someone, you can see the facial expressions that tell me if this person is lying—just overall seeing people's expressions as something happens.

The Impact of Entering a Story World

Because they were able to enter the story worlds through their senses, reading became, as Frijda might have predicted, an opportunity to be "immersed in emotions of different sorts" (p. 79). Here's Helen talking about just that:

> I just get mad at them sort of. Sometimes I find myself yelling in my mind at characters in a book, like "No! Why would you do that?" especially when you know more than they do as you're reading. Kind of like people who talk to the TV when they're watching soap operas. "No, Travis, don't do it!"

We see this emotion in Michelle's read-aloud of Kenneth Oppel's *Starclimber*, part of the Matt Cruse series:

> "'Marry me,' I said." And he actually asked her that before at the beginning of the book but she said no. He was like heartbroken, and so I am like, "Yes, you should say yes!" I don't know how to explain that, I guess, just like, hooray!

Michelle's "hooray" indicates just how intense her engagement with the characters is.

Other readers elaborated on this engagement. Here's Rebecca talking about the pleasure she gets from having been part of the characters' lives in a series:

> They become like your friends. And you're so much in their lives they're like your best friends. And then you go to the next series and then you have a new best friend. But then you're like, "Oh my god! My old best friend is still here with me!" And most of the time when you start a new book you don't get to do that because it's a new series. None of the characters [you already know] are gonna be there. It's a different story altogether.

Paul made a similar point in an exchange with Jeff:

JEFF: *Now, do you feel like you've got kind of a relationship with the characters and you like reading about their next adventures and reading about one book helps you read the next one?*

PAUL: *I kind of feel like that, yeah. I've kind of grown up with Tintin my whole life so I kind of know the character. Which is kind of a good character to fall back on.*

JEFF: *What do you mean by that, a good character to fall back on?*

PAUL: *Like it's just a character that you know really well and you know their exploits and it's just kind of fun to watch them again, do something so it's like a character that doesn't grow old. Like in the next scene or book.*

Our participants were also emotionally involved with the characters in their games as Christian revealed:

> I felt exhilarated as well, and like, "Oh thank goodness he's not stuck on that mountain." But he was safe after a while. He got off the train, but we don't know what's going to happen next. I still feel kind of worried about him, but it's like oh, okay, I guess he's safe.

THE TEXTUAL CONTEXTS THAT PROVIDE PLAY PLEASURE

As the quotes we've already shared show, many of our participants saw fantasy as a particularly good genre for providing the pleasure of play. Alex articulated just why that is so:

> I really like science fiction and fantasy just in general, mainly because it's a way to get away from the world, and it's somewhere that you can't be, so it's like you can go there mentally not necessarily physically. It's like with realistic fiction, it's something that could happen any day, but with like a science fiction or fantasy it's not something that will just randomly happen every day.

So, too, did Alex:

> I think kind of the thing with the whole sci-fi/fantasy is that it's not realistic fiction where it can happen, it might happen. The fantasy thing, a completely different world that you can't go to physically, but you can go there mentally. It's like an alternate universe.

And Michelle: "I think it can take you somewhere new. I mean completely new. I mean you never have a chance to see this world again, except for in this book."

Regardless of genre, our participants were outspoken about the importance of a strong narrative thread. When asked the kind of books he likes, Terry responded:

> Suspenseful action. I personally am really into war books like . . . *Lone Survivor* by Marcus Luttrell. It's a story of a navy seal who survived an attack. I read those because it keeps me involved, and it's true, and it's just action, action, action and it makes me want to keep reading.

John agreed:

> *The Kite Runner* by Khaled Hosseini was a pretty interesting story of how diversity was changed and how Afghanistan was before the Taliban came through and how war affected it and the Soviets came down. I thought that was a very interesting book to see how one kid grew up and how he was a brother to his best friend. Then it got really action-packed when he had to go back to Afghanistan and be disguised. I think that was the best part. It was just what I was looking for.

The building up of action is what attracted Alex to J. R. R. Tolkien's *The Lord of the Rings*:

> I think it's building, going along, kind of solving problems going through, traveling, and seeing different regions of this world the author's created. Just that kind of building, building, building, building, building, and it's a story that builds and builds as the quest goes on and on and then more things begin to happen as you go. And then, once you finally reach that point where Gollum falls off the edge of the cliff with the ring, and the ring is destroyed, the end, it's like you build up build up build up and it's just like that kind of feeling of that accomplishment.

Alex was so enamored of action that he packaged some canonical texts in surprising ways:

> I'd heard about *Beowulf* and *The Odyssey* and *The Iliad* and I was interested in reading those. I'll actually be reading *The Odyssey* this summer. I was kinda interested cuz I'd heard the titles a couple times, and I was curious . . . And then I heard it was kinda a lot about action, cuz I like the—I like reading about that. And it also had the giants, and the dragon, and that kind of equates out to fantasy but deployed out in such a way it's almost not.

Once again, what was true of books was true of games. When Jeff asked Christian, "Are there times where you would choose one game over the other?" Christian responded,

"Yeah there's definitely times where I'm looking at my game library and I'm saying I don't want to play that one because it's a little too slow at times, but I'll play that one because I really want to be in the action."

THE POSSIBILITY OF ESCAPE

The pleasures of play that we've discussed in this chapter had a real pay-off for our participants. Most importantly, they deeply enjoyed their reading and gaming as a consequence. And, as Alex explained in an exchange with Jeff, that enjoyment brought corollary benefits, the kind of absorption Nell chronicles:

> **ALEX:** *[Reading provides a] kind of enjoyment, to get away to a new world almost. New places and things.*
>
> **JEFF:** *Okay, so when you say get away from the world around you, what do you mean by that?*
>
> **ALEX:** *So, say you're like at school, you're doing work and everything. You get home, and you're just, like, kind of tired of being at school and having to think about all this, so you can just sit down and read, you know? Just completely forget about everything else that's going on and just be totally into the story.*

That forgetting can be therapeutic, as Callie explained: "Oh yeah, even if it's just to be able to get away and be completely absorbed for an hour, it does make my life easier." Rori expressed a similar sentiment: "Well, I usually read the most when I'm like really mad or if I'm really sad because it's a way of escape for me." So did Rebecca:

> Reading at home, it's to stop being angry. When I get angry, I'm like, "Rrrrr," and I can't stop. I just have to stop thinking about it and I eventually forget. So I read a book or just sit there and listen to music, but mostly it's books. I read a book and I just like go into the book and be there. So it's just a way to go away from what's actually happening in the real world and just be there.

A Word About Intensity, Timing, and Duration

We think the quotes we've shared help you see just how intense the pleasure of play was for our readers. Look, for example, at the language Michelle used in an exchange with Jeff:

MICHELLE: *Yes, I read this really great book, uh, I just finished the sequel but it was* City of Bones *. . . . It had the most amazing twists that I never would have thought of, ever. And it seemed very probable but it was like crazy how well she hid them until the right time. And I just read the sequel that also had some really great twists.*

JEFF: *Which is?*

MICHELLE: City of Ashes.

JEFF: *Oh, okay.*

MICHELLE: *I think you might know those. Yeah, they are pretty big; they are really addicting. So now I have all of these kinds of like theories how this guy isn't actually her brother.*

JEFF: *So, you think you're gonna continue to be surprised in the third book?*

MICHELLE: *Yeah, I'm really waiting for it to come in at the library; I'm like thirteen in line so that's kind of sad.*

The book is "really great," "amazing," and "addicting," an intense experience indeed.

Although the pleasure of play was primarily experienced while our readers were reading, series books allowed our readers to extend their pleasure through the anticipatory pleasure of getting the next book. Our readers also extended the duration of their pleasure in three other ways, what Nell (1988) calls "savoring" (p. 112), rereading, and remembering. By savoring, Nell means slowing down during a reader's favorite parts. Our readers talked about doing this at the end of books they especially enjoyed. Here's Alex:

[If] there's a book I really like, I don't want to finish it. I just want to keep going cuz it's a book that I really like throughout the entire book, and I don't want it to be over. It's like you finish it and it's like well, what's next? What happens now?

When Jeff asked Helen if she ever slowed down at the end of a book, he got a surprising answer:

> I actually have a book right now that I'm a couple pages away from the end and I stopped reading it [and] said, "No I will not finish it."

If she finishes it, the pleasure ends.

But once you finish, you can still reread. The pleasure of play continues even in rereading as Michelle explained:

> Yes, I really love [rereading]. Probably just as much as when I first know it's going to happen. Because even the second time, I already know it's going to happen but I get really caught up in it anyway, again. And it's like I don't know what's going to happen all over again. Like, I know it's there in the back of my mind but, it's still exciting.

Helen made a similar comment:

> I'll only reread books I'll really like, and, I really like a lot of books. Rereading them, it's not the same as when I first read them, it's, it's just remembering my favorite parts as I go along. It's kind of nice to know what's gonna happen.

But even if she doesn't reread, she can still remember. When Jeff asked her why she chose the scene she chose for her think-aloud, she responded,

HELEN: *Because it's one I come back to a lot.*

JEFF: *What do you get coming back to it?*

HELEN: *Just a little bit of the sense of silliness. And it just reminds me of the rest of the story and how the book is written. So I can carry around this scene and the rest of the book with me without having to sit and actually read the book. Just have to remind myself every once in a while.*

In short, the pleasure of play was so intense our readers didn't want to give it up.

WHAT WE CAN LEARN FROM OUR READERS' PLAY PLEASURE

We're going to conclude our book by thinking about the implications of our study, but we also wanted to conclude each chapter by highlighting a couple of findings that we think are especially compelling. We found ourselves enormously moved by our participants' explanation of what happens when they enter a story world. Our data pleases us, therefore, when we reflect on the kinds of instruction we have promoted over many years that engages students in doing just that. Jeff, for example, (Smith & Wilhelm, 2006; Wilhelm 2008, 2012c; Wilhelm & Edmiston, 1998) has long-championed drama as the most powerful way for students to enter stories. Dramatic techniques like in-role writing, good angel/bad angel, hot seating, and alter ego encourage and reward all students for entering story worlds in the way these committed readers do.

But not all reading emphasizes the power of entering a story world. We've long thought that Vipond and Hunt's (1984) discrimination among three different orientations towards reading (information-driven readings, story-driven readings, and point-driven readings) is particularly useful to teachers and researchers for thinking about different approaches to reading because of its clarity and simplicity.

According to Vipond and Hunt (1984), information-driven reading "is especially appropriate in learning-from-text situations where content is relevant" (p. 268), story-driven readings "tend to emphasize plot, character, and event" (p. 269), and point-driven reading concerns "the sharing and comparing of values and beliefs" (p. 263). We realize that as committed as we are to the power of story, we have tended to see these orientations as hierarchic, with point-driven reading being the most important. Even a quick look at the emphases of the Common Core State Standards Reading Anchor Standard 2: "Determine central ideas or themes of a text and analyze their development; summarize the key supporting details and ideas" establishes that we're far from alone. Our data convince us that we always need to be more mindful of the power of story and of the play and pleasure of reading.

Such mindfulness makes us examine some of the instructional decisions we have made in the past. Michael admits that he never assigned students a thriller or mystery or fantasy. Jeff's been better, due largely to his emphasis on free-choice reading, but he, too, has emphasized nuanced, realistic texts when the class is reading the same book.

Our data also make us wonder about some strategies that are very common. Do reading logs or dialogue journals interfere with entering a story world by bringing kids back from the world of the narrative to the world of school? Michelle thought so:

> I think my least favorite assignment would be the ones where we have to, we have like reading journals; and we're supposed to pull out like certain things from them or like, you need to put things down about the plot and any questions you have. . . . And I have to stop my reading to do that.

We wonder how she'd feel about our interrupting the reading of a text to ask clarifying questions or to share our interpretation through a think-aloud. We understand more fully now that we need to weigh the benefits of such interruptions against their costs. The articulate responses of our participants convince us that it would be worth asking the students with whom we work to weigh in with their opinions on the instructional choices we make. The pleasure of play is powerful in and of itself, but also in the foundation it lays for crucially important work. We want to do all we can to protect the pleasure of play.

CHAPTER 4

WORK PLEASURE

"This Is It!"

When we were working on *Reading Don't Fix No Chevys*, we were pretty confident that we were collecting good data. But we worried because none of the books and articles we were reading seemed to be useful in explaining those data. But when we read Mihaly Csikszentmihalyi's (1990) *Flow: The Psychology of Optimal Experience*, we knew we had found what we were looking for. An excited email from Michael to Jeff: "You have to read this book." An excited response from Jeff: "This is it!" We took enormous pleasure in that reading because the book was so useful in helping us think about something important to us.

What we experienced was what we are calling the pleasure of work, a kind of pleasure that's distinct from the immersive pleasure of play that our readers experienced by entering a story world. Work pleasure is the pleasure one takes from using a text as a tool to accomplish something. As you'll see, the ends that our readers were seeking to accomplish were not those instrumental ends discussed by policy makers. For the most part, our readers weren't thinking about college and career. They had much more immediate and personally compelling goals.

Dewey (1916) provides an explanation for our readers' emphasis on the immediate when he writes that, "children proverbially live in the present." He notes further that young people's focus on the here and now "is not only a fact not to be evaded, but it is an excellence!" (p. 55). He continues:

Healthy work, done for present reasons and as a factor in living, is largely unconscious. The stimulus resides in the situation with which one is actually confronted. But when this situation is ignored, pupils have to be told that if they do not follow the prescribed course, penalties will accrue; while if they do, they may expect, some time in the future, rewards for their present sacrifices. Everybody knows how largely systems of punishment have had to be resorted to by educational systems which neglect present possibilities in behalf of preparation for the future. (pp. 55–56)

Our readers embraced the present possibilities reading provides. They clearly took pleasure in the healthy work that they were doing. That's why it's important to understand that what we mean by work does not stand in opposition to what we mean by play. We think this is an important enough point that it's worth sharing an extended example of Dewey's (1913) analysis that contextualizes a quote we shared in Chapter 2:

There seems to be no better name for the acts of using intermediate means, or appliances, to reach ends than work. When employed in this way, however, work must be distinguished from labor and from toil and drudgery. Labor means a form of work in which the direct result accomplished is of value only as a means of exchange for something else. It is an economic term, being applied to that form of work where the product is paid for, and the money paid is used for objects of more direct values. Toil implies unusual arduousness in a task, involving fatigue. Drudgery is an activity which in itself is quite disagreeable, performed under the constraint of some quite extraneous need. Play and work cannot, therefore, be distinguished from one another according to the presence or absence of direct interest in what is doing. A child engaged in making something with tools, say, a boat, may be just as immediately interested in what he is doing as if he were sailing the boat. He is not doing what he does for the mere sake of an external result—the boat—nor for the mere sake of sailing it later. The thought of the finished product and of the use to which it is to be put may come to his mind, but so as to enhance his immediate activity of construction. (pp. 78–79)

The uses to which students put their reading were of two fundamentally different sorts. On the one hand, they experienced the pleasure of work to accomplish practical ends. On the other, they experienced the pleasure of work to address deeply personal issues in what might be called inner work. We coded nearly 300 content units as relating to these kinds of work pleasures.

Taking Pleasure in the Practical

One of the practical work pleasures our students sought was using reading to progress in their writing. Indeed, the prevalence of this pleasure was one of our most surprising findings.

Reading as Writers

Here's Rebecca talking about how her reading provides grist for her future writing:

> [I read to] discover new stuff to add to what I will eventually create as my ultimate story of epic doom. Yes. Epic doom. [I read to get] ideas for the plot of my epic story of epic doom. That I will eventually create, and it is in the process of being created as I already have pretty much all of the characters that I will ever use. I might add a few more later on. Maybe. But I already have like a hundred so that might not be a very good idea. Dot dot dot.

And later:

> That's why I read fan fiction. Not only do I write it but I read it. Because if I didn't read it then I wouldn't be very good at writing it probably, and then I wouldn't get new theories. Cuz in other people's fan fictions they have these ideas that they all made and I go into them and I read them and I'm like that's ingenious! And then I go and I alter it a little bit and then I add it into mine.

Michelle made a similar point in an exchange with Jeff:

MICHELLE: *Well, I like reading books that I can write about. Like I'm very interested in writing government conspiracy stories, so I like to pull things from other books and I can kind of think, "Okay, well this worked really well in this story so how can I do something like that in a book I am writing?"*

JEFF: *So you read like a writer?*

MICHELLE: *Yes, I don't think I ever read like a reader. I'm not sure what that really means, but I'm always thinking about okay, this character needs a character change about in the next few scenes because otherwise this plot isn't going to keep going. And, I'm usually right but the more I think about that, the more picky I* *get about books. And like, if I see how flat a main character is I get very annoyed with them and I get kind of annoyed with the writer that they didn't give them a character arc or anything.*

Karen joined the chorus:

For writing I think about why do I like this book so much and why do I want to read it and I think about what the author is doing . . . and how could I apply this to my writing that would make other people want to read it? . . . I always have trouble writing intros. So I started paying a lot more attention to what an author was doing in the intro that I really liked and why I liked it so much so I have used some of those elements before or maybe I just thought about them. Then there were other times when I got this whole new view from a book and I guess I kind of applied it to what I did.

In response to the question "Anything else that you've learned?" she continued:

I like in, I forget which book, but he started out really small and then he went kind of big. You didn't exactly know what was going to happen. You just explained some detail, I forget what it was. Just like a small object and explained it in a really descriptive way and then he kind of zoomed out to the whole scene. I really liked how he did that.

Alex also spoke of how she used her reading to advance her writing:

I think [reading] also helps in writing ability, too, because it helps like in *The Sight*, there's that really good description. I know when I read and I come across words that I don't use very often and maybe I don't really understand, I try to remember those words and use them in my writing, you know, just kind of up the vocabulary level of your writing. And then also it kind of gives you that idea of like, okay, so the way that this is written gives me that mental image. How can I try to use that type of mental, that way of writing the mental image? Kind of make it my own way.

She talked further about why she pays attention to a writer's craft:

Because I'm a writer myself and I think it helps as a writer to read other writers' work, because then it helps give you ideas, and different ways of doing things because if you never looked at the way other people do it, you're going to do whatever it is how you do it just the same way, and you're

> not going to change it. So after a while it's going to get, the same old same old, the way you're writing it's just going to be the same way you're writing. But, when you have the different elements and ideas you can really kind of change it up.

And later:

> You can bring elements from different types of books into [your writing]. And so, you can pull in that information, like with *The Sight* it does have some historical background in it, too, with some of the wars that go on between man in it. And like, the colonization of the Romanian area and things like that. And some also of the folklore, the old Romanian folklore is in it. So, it's kind of pulling those different elements from different genres into a fantasy, and that gives a different edge. So it does help to have those different genres, like ideas the way things are written in it.

Unlike the students who had thought of themselves as writers for some time, Callie's recent reading had encouraged her to start:

> So when I started reading Palahniuk I started writing my own short stories and like it's just a nicer way to look at the world when you can find the comedy in the darkness, and I think that's one of the main things I get from that author.

Instead of being a fiction writer, John was a blogger on current events. He read not so much to get stylistic pointers but rather to find content:

> I blogged about just news and to share my ideas of what happens when certain conflicts come into our government. Let's just say Watergate, and how that affected Pakistan, and now if that happened again, which it seems to be repeating itself sometimes in our government, I just see it from the point of view and made the connections. So I just looked at the history pretty much.

In short, many of our readers used their reading as tool to help them develop as writers. And they took pleasure from being able to do so.

Reading as Talkers

One of our favorite findings of our *Reading Don't Fix No Chevys* study (2002) is the importance of what we called "exportability." That is, the young men in our study took pleasure from reading something they could export into conversation. So, too, did these readers.

Not all of John's current event reading was focused on his blogging. He also read to inform his face-to-face conversations as he explained with reference to the Palestinian-Israeli conflict:

JOHN: *I like to stay aware of worldwide issues. . . . From one side of the story you could be out of a different religion and the writer could be saying this from one religion, like an example would be the Palestine conflict. The Palestinian-Israeli conflict. You can see it from the Palestinian side, you can see the whole points of their side, but then you can also read it from the Israeli [side] and see what they're seeing and feeling. So the emotion between two sides is the conflict. And then sometimes you can read from the* New York Times, *reading about those two conflicts and see how they clash and how that's affecting the world.*

JEFF: *Why is this in-depth exploration so important?*

JOHN: *Well your argument's gonna get proven wrong if you don't see the other side, cuz if you're just speaking at one side, nobody's gonna want to listen to you. You have to be able to acknowledge both sides of any conflict or purpose, to figure out what to do basically, and how to organize your side. . . .Just [to] express your ideas, you pretty much need both sides.*

Callie's interest in dark fiction was in part because of its conversational benefits:

But beyond that, with the knowledge I gained from these books, when I get into conversations and/or arguments with people, I have a perspective that they wouldn't usually see, so when we get into these conversations and/or arguments I can bring out that and make them consciously think about how we are the future. We don't really have to tolerate failed political regimes and corporate America destroying our future and limiting our possibilities. Dark fiction opened up endless possibilities but they're set in a realistic point.

Helen talked about the authority such conversational preparation provides:

And then, using it? I guess I just have a lot of the stuff, just sort of in my brain and then when that kind of subject comes up, they'll need the information I have. And then, I can usually just tell people, "Oh, I just read this book, and it turns out yadda-ya" or sometimes I won't even tell them I read the book. I'll just say, "Did you know?" or "Oh I heard about that."

Reading as Thinkers

Our readers experienced work pleasure in what they learned while they read even if that knowledge never made it into a conversation. Here's John:

> When you're on a long flight you have to read to keep yourself awake. So I get some good out of the flight. I'll bring a couple books and read them and then if the flight's still going on for another four hours I'll read them again. I'll look at them from different perspectives. That's how crazy it is. I basically just learn off what I read all day.

Wesley made a similar point:

> Well I see it as sort of a way to learn and entertain yourself quietly, and you can do it over a long period of time instead of like, what some people do playing video games is they play the entire game in two hours and then get bored with it. With a book you can read it, enjoy it for a long period of time because you have to actually think about what you're reading. Like, I make connections with the text and think about other things that the book has to deal with when I read. And like I said before it's also a way to learn stuff. Many books are about different things, so you can learn a lot from just reading fiction books or historical fiction, or even nonfiction books.

Terry especially valued the knowledge he could learn about other people:

> I like to understand people better than what I could do in real life. Like I can't, as I said, stick a tube up your brain and know what you're thinking. When people write books . . . , you can know what they were thinking at the time, what they recount they were thinking.

Interestingly, when our readers talked about games they made similar points about the importance of using games to learn. Some of their learning was factual, as Wesley indicated in talking about *Assassin's Creed 2*:

> It has the locations and they are real and you get history like about Santa Trinita [a church in Florence]. So you learn about all this architecture and its history and it can help you with the story and playing the game.

But sometimes what they learned goes far beyond facts, as Robert explained:

> And also video games, we also have to keep in mind, like, as I said before, it opens up the new possibility factor and you have to wonder like, what does this show us in a way? Because I think it's, as I said, very important to find, to put meaning in the game, or a point of maybe, if you make a war game, make a point that war is terrifying, and there's fear and sadness and sorrow in it, not just it's happy to go around shooting people.

Reading as Doers

Our readers not only sought knowledge for the sake of knowledge, they also sought knowledge that had an immediate functional use. The most avid gamers spoke about how some of their reading supported their gaming. Robert explained why he wants to read gaming magazines:

> You always kinda want to know what's gonna be the next big step in gaming, what's gonna be really amazing and new. There's almost always something like that. There's always a new singularity approaching that will change video games forever. . . . I also just look for what's interesting to me, what would I want to play. Also just keeping aware of what's out there. I mean, I would look at an old one and say, "Oh, I didn't know that game was out. I should look for it. It sounds interesting."

So did Terry:

> I like to read the reviews so I can know which games I'd like to rent, because normally I rent a game before I buy it unless I already know it's going to be awesome . . . . *Game Informer* had a whole magazine devoted to [*Modern Warfare 2*] before it came out, and this was before I decided to preorder. I read the reviews, I read all about it, and that got me really hyped up. I was really excited to buy this game. I think the next day I went into Gamestop and I preordered it, and I paid for the game so as soon as it came out I could pick up my copy and not have to pay or anything.

Christian read *Game Informer* religiously every month:

> I'm expecting my new issues this week. I skip around for the games I am interested in. Particularly previews. Then I go back to the interviews.

> They give insights into the why of the game and the story [behind what] motivated it and the characters and it makes the game I am playing more interesting.

He also read strategy guides:

> These are guides that help you through—guides are bigger than the manuals—about the whole games—lots of tips—for when you need help. If the game is tough and frustrating, I will use them a lot. Or if there is secret stuff I want to know about. All games have Easter Eggs and secret things. Easter Eggs are quirky secrets—you do this certain thing and a cow might move, like in pinball, so it is funny.

In short, far from being in competition with reading, gaming provided incentives to engage in it.

Our readers also talked about reading as preparation for the future, though that was a decidedly less significant form of work pleasure. In an exchange with Jeff, Paul talked about how his future plans affected his current reading:

JEFF: *Now why do you want to be an archeologist?*

PAUL: *I really enjoy history like ancient history and, I don't know, just studying ancient history would be cool.*

JEFF: *How does that play in, if it all, to your reading interests?*

PAUL: *Well, I do like books with some historical facts in them, like some actual facts in it . . . so it's not a complete shot in the dark, but those are really cool, too.*

If reading might be useful in the future, great. But "it's really cool" even if it doesn't survive into the future.

Callie was more fanciful in speaking of her future plans in an exchange with Jeff:

CALLIE: *There's this book that I'm currently reading that's about cadavers and crime scene investigation and stuff, and it's really technical about that, but because it's so weird and you won't hear about it, and it's nice to think about what you'll never really know about in any other circumstance.*

JEFF: *Why is that so important to you?*

CALLIE: *I think because there'll be some point in my life where I'll relate* *to it, like maybe I'll get involved with the mob, or maybe I'll end up on a crime scene at some point. Having that background, it makes you think about the possibilities of your life, and it makes you find connections where usually you wouldn't.*

One hopes that Callie won't find this reading as useful as she thinks it might be. But she found pleasure in the possibility.

The Pleasure of Inner Work

Thus far we've seen that our readers consciously employed their reading as a tool to do immediate and important work in the world. Reading helped our participants be better writers, better talkers and thinkers, and better gamers. It provided them with richer understandings of the world outside themselves. It also helped them to do inner work.

"Inner work," according to Jungian scholar Robert Johnson (1986), "is the effort by which we gain an awareness of the deeper layers of consciousness within us and move to an integration of the total self" (p. 13). The unconscious, according to Jung, expresses itself through symbol, story, and feeling. Jung argued that the two primary modes the unconscious uses to communicate with the conscious mind are through dreams and through imagination. Jung maintained that when we approach the unconscious and embrace its messages, cultivating our receptivity and response to the language of symbolism, we lead healthier, fuller, more wide-awake, balanced, and richer lives.

The notion that reading can be inner work, a spiritual practice, a way to profound and deepened ways of growing as human beings is not a new idea. The rule for monasteries established throughout Egypt and the Middle East by the Coptic Saint Pachomius maintained that the candidates for monkhood "shall be compelled to read." Benedictine rule likewise sets aside a period each day for "prayerful reading" (Greenblatt, 2011, p. 25).

The understanding that reading can provide an avenue for personal growth is something we've long argued for both separately and together (Rabinowitz & Smith, 1998; Smith & Wilhelm, 2010, Wilhelm & Novak, 2011). We've drawn on Wayne Booth's (1988) argument that "We all live a great proportion of our lives in a surrender to stories about our lives, and about other possible lives" (p. 14). Readers are able to learn about possible lives because, as Booth explains, stories are typically centered on characters' grappling in some way or another with moral choices. In living through those efforts, "we readers stretch our own capacities for thinking about how life should be lived" (p. 187). Bruner (1986) makes a similar argument, claiming that narratives allow one to traffic "in human possibilities rather than in settled certainties" (p. 26).

In one of our favorite quotes, Coles (1989) provides a moving testimony to Booth's and Bruner's position by sharing a student's remarks about the power of story:

> *When I have some big moral issue, some question to tackle, I think I try to remember what my folks have said, or I imagine them in my situation—or even more these days I think of [characters in books I've read]. Those folks, they're people for me . . . they really speak to me—there's a lot of me in them, or vice versa. I don't know how to put it, but they're voices, and they help me make choices. I hope when I decide "the big ones" they'll be in there pitching. (p. 203)*

We've often used this quote in our writing about discussions of the power of story. So imagine our delight in reading this remark of Helen's:

Sometimes when, like, big stuff happens in my life, I'll think about what my favorite character would have done, the ones I admire most. Also, sort of subconscious; I don't stop and think about what someone would do, it's just something that happens. Like, I bet so-and-so would be really brave about this, or, one of my favorite characters would have totally sped after this guy. And then sometimes I follow their example and sometimes I don't. . . . They all have different approaches, different ways they approach things, and then I try to apply that to my life, to see which way works for me. Characters are just ways of thinking, really.

Michelle made a similar point:

You can look to books, I think, and characters for their influences. Also I think a psychology kind of thing. You can look at oh, so I made a mistake like that so that could be why they reacted that way and realized also how the characters reacted in real life, you know? Maybe I shouldn't have done that. And you can reference your own experiences off books. And you can kind of "Yeah, so I shouldn't do that again because the character also found that very offensive." Kind of like a cautionary buddy.

So, too, did Alex:

When I read I kind of find a character that I relate to the most. I kind of watch them through the book, just because having a character that's so much of yourself, kind of following the character along through events and the problems and [unclear] so it kind of, the problem comes up, and you kind of have that, you feel more like you can handle it. You're thinking about where you connect. And also at the end, I usually do look back and think about it because I am very reflective when I read anyways.

Helen, Michelle, and Alex weren't alone in their conscious awareness of the inner work their reading allowed them to do. Callie was amazingly articulate about how the dark fiction that comprised the bulk of her out-of-school reading made her conscious of different possibilities for how she makes decisions and lives her life:

It influences how I respond to a situation. So if I were responding to a situation in a fiction state of mind, I would probably be like the teen heroine in this fiction state of mind where something horrible happens to them, but then they emotionally grow and strive above it. That's my fiction voice. But a more realistic dark character, something really horrible happens and I have no idea what to do and I think and I ponder about what the possibilities are as I try and try desperately to overcome this situation but never really do and end up moving on with this situation that still is left hanging. Like, because that's a way more realistic way of life. Say your cat dies. The teen heroine would cry for three days, and then overcome it and help comfort her little sister. Then the dark fiction character would be like, "What happened to the cat? Why did the cat die? This is horrible." So they would be sad, but they would be so concerned about why the cat died that they wouldn't really have a chance to respond to the sadness, and that would be the underlying tone of the dark fiction as they respond to how the cat died.

And later:

I think the books give me a way that I can see the possibilities of how to respond, because like Misty [from *Palahniuk's Diary*] failed and if you got here you've failed and so then like I think about how, in a possibility like that, I would try to, like, it gives me more possibilities of how I can respond. Like, she responded and she tried and she tried and she still failed. I'm going to keep trying, even if I fail. That kind of made me think about what if I still fail, and then like other books they make you think about like what could you do, what should you do. Should you run from your fear and should you run from all the stuff you have, or should you keep trying?

Callie spun out a specific example of how her reading influenced her living when she talked about how *Invisible Monsters* affected her:

It talks a lot about parents and how parents are like God . . . and how once you become a teenager you become Satan because you want to find something better. It was a very weird book, but at that time I was having some fights with my mom, so when I started thinking about that and thinking about how to, like, the knowledge I learned from the book was pretty introspective about how parents see their child and how kids see their parents and the complexes that go on both ways, and so when I started thinking about that and thinking about my mom and how we both handle the situations, it became a lot easier to understand. And so I think applying it to my life, and even just getting away from my life, it makes it easier.

And later:

But it was all about beauty image, and this supermodel who ends up in a really horrible accident and her face gets horribly disfigured, but she was a supermodel before that. And so it's kind of about her life afterwards. It really questions beauty industry standards, and it questions how the world relates to beauty and how we ourselves respond to beauty. And so, as a teenage girl, there's always that air of self-consciousness. And so as I was thinking back on that book a few weeks later as I was looking in the mirror and I'm like "Wow I really could lose a few pounds," but then I was thinking back on that book and I was like "Well, that's not the key part of my life." I was thinking back on that book and it questioned the reality of what we leave ourselves with when we completely remake ourselves and I'm like, maybe if I wasn't this I wouldn't be this person. It made me think about myself and then it made me be a little more positive about who I am or how I am. I related to that book after I read it in a way that I didn't relate to it as I was reading it. And I used that to help me with beauty image.

And finally:

I think more than shaping my identity [dark fiction] shapes my perception of reality because a lot of these books question reality so it shapes my perception of reality and my perception of the world, which in turn shapes me because if I perceive the world in a set way then I will perceive myself in that definition of how the world should be perceived. But if I perceive the world as a place with so many different dimensions and possibilities and the way people relate to each other, like, if I perceive the world that way then I can perceive myself in a completely different way than if I was so set on how the world is perceived by popular society.

Other genres played similar roles in other readers' lives. We'll be talking about Harry Potter at great length in a separate chapter, but we think it's worth noting now that the Harry Potter fans used those books in a manner similar to the ways in which Callie used her dark fiction. Here's Michelle:

I think Harry Potter is kind of interesting. . . . He had a lot of anger issues. And he is actually a very annoying character. I don't like him very much but I related a lot to him. He was always ducking responsibilities and you know putting things off and then later somehow turning around and being the heroic one. It's like an unlikely hero kind of, even though it was kind of like his destiny to save the world from Voldemort. It was like he wasn't completely found, by that I mean he messed up and got Sirius killed and stuff so it's not like he has this plan in his mind; he like makes it up as he goes along and I think that's how I live my life a lot._

Mia was also a fan. Although she related to a different character, that relating did a similar kind of work, as the following exchange with Jeff reveals:

MIA: *I think the fantasy character that I compare most with would be Ron from Harry Potter.*

JEFF: *Now why do you relate to him, and how do you use him to think with?*

MIA: *Well cuz we both don't really do stuff very good. Like, we're both kinda clumsy. And he doesn't like people who are like stuck up. Like I don't.*

JEFF: *So you kinda share some personal traits with him. And you also share some values. So are you ever in a situation where you think what would Ron do?*

MIA: *Yes.*

JEFF: *Can you tell us a situation where that might be the case?*

MIA: *Well like, I was about to go take [a test], and I was thinking should I panic, or should I not panic? Ron would panic. But I don't think that would be good since it's a Spanish [test].*

JEFF: *So you actually learned something not to do.*

Alex went so far as creating quote books, so she would have them on hand when she needed them:

ALEX: *Well when I read anything I'm like, I'm kind of nicknamed the "Quotes Queen" because in every book I read, I'll find at least like ten quotes, at least. I just like see quotes. You know I just pop out and I'm like, "Oh hey, there's a quote and that fits in life" and so it's just kind of a thing, the way I read it anyways. I just see quotes when I read.*

JEFF: *Can you talk about that?*

ALEX: *Just reading and you read a line and you're like, "Oh, wow, that describes maybe something in my life" or something you know, maybe something I could use later in life or maybe just a good message. Just on a way to live or something.*

JEFF: *And do you, so you write these down. Do you ever think about them or use them?*

ALEX: *I think about them and use them as often as I can.*

Michael was particularly struck by Alex's work because in his high school days, he was a quote collector, too, though he wrote them on his army surplus jacket instead of in a book. Over 40 years later he can still see Yeats's "What the world's million lips are thirsting for/Must be substantial somewhere" on the left-hand pocket of his jacket.

Quite clearly, our readers used texts as tools to help them discover who they are, to become more conscious of possibilities, and to imaginatively rehearse and try out these possibilities. Michelle made that point explicitly:

> I kind of think about how characters are always influenced and sometimes I think maybe that's pretty good and sometimes that's not any better. So I guess it all depends and I look at a situation very carefully. Now it's okay, if I respond like I usually do, is that better than if I responded in a different way? I guess that's not who I am, but I guess [reading] helps me discover who I am kind of.

Or could be. Bruner notes that narratives can do more than teach us who we are. They can also teach us who we might be. Our readers also recognized that power. Here's Robert:

> I think it is very important to have something that's very intense because that's one thing that wants you to keep reading and it keeps you paying attention to the story in the book, and that's one thing that, you kind of know a story's very good when it has that bright intensity to it. And so if you read something like *Les Mis* it has those points. I mean, it's such a long book and it has all this description but that's kind of what makes it intense because he has very vivid descriptions of like the people dying on the streets of the cities and everything happening around you, and so you have to. I think that that's very important to have, so yeah I'd say that schools need to look for books that have that intensity and that there it is, you have to think what if I was there? What if I was in that situation?

Helen made a similar point in an extended exchange with Jeff:

JEFF: *Do you think you ever learn something from a character that you make a part of your personality?*

HELEN: *Yeah, I guess. Like, when they overreact or underreact or something to a certain situation, and then you think about how cool it would be to be them, and then you remember how much they screwed up at that one part, and then you remember, "I will not do that." So then I can't be them and live their life, because I know that that was stupid.*

JEFF: *I'm wondering if you could think of an example where after you read a book, maybe you felt different, or thought something had shifted inside you.*

HELEN: *There's those books about people, like, overcoming great evil under horrible odds and stuff. And it makes you think about how many risks you're taking in your life and stuff. Like, in* The Lord of the Rings, *Frodo, whoa. He sacrificed so much for everybody else, and he was just a normal guy, hobbit, thing. And, you can kind of idolize him almost, thinking about how he saved Middle Earth. I think, well, if, I dunno, my town was in danger but not immediately for me, would I go do something really heroic to save the world, pretty much? And, also, the kind of books,*

the author and the characters do have problems along the
way on their great quest, and that makes me think the whole
perseverance thing. But you don't think about it at the time.
And it's almost better not to have to think about it at the time.

JEFF: *But you're saying it somehow gets deep inside you.*

HELEN: *Mm-hmm.*

She continued later:

> Well, I learn about myself through books when I imagine myself in the
> different situations. I'm pretty sure other people do that, too. And then I
> really can think about what would I really do. Would I run and hide or would
> I, you know, stand up and take it? And then you say well I like to think that I
> would stay, but maybe I really would run away and the next time you've got
> that fight or flight thing going on, you kinda think back to which one you
> want to be doing. You can sort of help yourself change in that way, and when
> you really admire a character in a book who's really brave and stuff, you kind
> of can idolize them and become more like them. So it's not really learning
> about yourself, it's learning about what you could be, sort of.

Helen also used characters as potential models:

> And, in the Tamora Pierce [books] there's a character named Ding, who's
> my favorite. Kind of a weird name. She has magic animal powers. She learns
> about herself all the time, and she's always learning about everything all
> the time. In the beginning of the book she's very meek and shy and then
> towards the end she's powerful and out there and it's just fun to watch her
> metamorphosis thing, and I guess I kind of relate to that little metamorphosis
> part of it cuz I'm way different than I was a few years ago. A lot of the times
> I like a character because I wish I was them. And then I sort of try and be a
> little more like the good parts of them.

Between us, we have devoted nearly 70 years to teaching, and we've been
particularly devoted to the teaching of narratives. We've long argued that stories offer
readers a unique and powerful way of knowing about themselves and about the world.
We've long believed both that stories can help individual students on their life journey
and that equipping students with the tools they need to navigate their lives in ever
more wide-awake and enriching ways should be our primary goals. But even we were

startled and moved by our readers' passionate recognition of the importance of their reading and their eloquent explanations of the work their reading allows them to do.

When we shared a draft of an early chapter of this book with our friend, the literary theorist Peter Rabinowitz, one of the comments he made was in response to this sentence from Chapter 2: "Maybe it's because we didn't want our readers to think of us as frivolous, especially in an era in which the focus of literacy education is so clearly college and career readiness." "That's right on target," he wrote. "*One* reason why we play down pleasure is that we want to appear 'serious' to those who are judging us (PhD advisors, state legislators, whomever). So what's the solution to this rhetorical/ political problem?" It's a hard question and an important one. But we think the testimonies provided by our readers in this chapter provide the beginning of an answer. Those testimonies help us see that the pleasure of work is serious business indeed— it's essential, solid work that should be valued and cultivated in developing readers.

A Word About Intensity, Timing, and Duration

Robert talked about how a book had to have "bright intensity" if it is to inspire inner work in which readers examine who they are and consider who they might be. The quotes we shared about inner work seem to us to have a bright intensity as well, an intensity that may even be greater than the intensity readers felt when they experienced the pleasures of play.

The pleasures of work also seem to be of longer duration. Readers experienced the pleasure of work as they were reading when they recognized that their reading would be useful for some future end. And they experienced it again when they employed their reading to achieving those ends. Sometimes those ends were instrumental. But in most cases even our readers regarded the reading that they did as a resource they could draw on again and again and again and again.

What We Can Learn From Our Readers' Work Pleasure

The pleasure our readers experienced in the different kinds of work that they did suggests to us that we should create classroom contexts that provide opportunities for as wide a variety of work as possible. We have regularly called for teachers to build their instruction around inquiry units that ask essential questions and to have those units culminate in some kind of composition as well as a social action project. Students could work together on the same social action project or they could devise their own. For example, as the culminating project for a unit centered around the question, "To what extent have sports had a positive influence on American life," two of Jeff's students made a formal appeal to the Board of Education. They suggested it would be wise to separate homecoming from a football game because of the negative effect sports sometimes has on American life. They argued that a football homecoming marginalized work that was more academic and artistic. Everything they read to help them make that argument had the capacity, then, to provide work pleasure.

Other possibilities abound. We see in this chapter that reading was pleasurable in part because it allowed students to communicate more effectively with a wider variety of audiences. Any activity, therefore, in which students can make their reading and their ideas about their reading public can provide a similar kind of pleasure. Students could create class blogs or wikis, or develop a gallery walk or webquest. In his teaching, Jeff often uses think-alouds, visualization and drama strategies, and reading manipulatives/symbolic story representations to help students make their reading processes and responses visible and available, and therefore shareable and able to do *work* with and for other students (see Wilhelm, 2008, 2012a, 2012b, 2012c for descriptions of this kind of work). The possibilities are endless.

Our readers also brought home to us the intimate relationship between reading and writing. But not writing of just any sort. The students who were writing fictional narratives of one sort or another took a kind of work pleasure from their reading that other readers didn't. We talk about the importance of narrative writing at length elsewhere (Fredricksen, Wilhelm, & Smith, 2012) and we argued previously (Smith & Wilhelm, 2010) about the importance of using "students' writing as a resource for their reading and vice versa" (p. 17). But, we have to admit, we see that importance even more clearly now.

However, the work that we found most powerful was the inner work that students did. Our suggestion here is a simple one: Make sure you never lose sight of why literature matters. Don't lose sight of what is uniquely powerful about transacting with literature. Remember Helen's line "Characters are just ways of thinking, really" and her intention to "try to be more like the good parts" of those characters. Remember Alex's cautionary buddies and her quote books. Remember how Callie's dark fiction helped her confront body image issues she was facing. If you keep such things in mind, you'll keep the focus not just on what texts mean but also on why they matter. You'll focus on the power of feeling and relational responding to the whole of human experience and to transformative possibilities for both individuals and groups. You'll engage students in activities in which they examine the moral choices characters make and think hard about what alternatives are available. You'll encourage them to respect the texts that they find moral and resist those they do not. This is all work that is well worth doing.

CHAPTER 5

Intellectual Pleasure

"It's Like Being a Detective Almost"

We've both been in book clubs for years and years. One reason we like participating so much is that we know that our interpretive questions, whatever they may be as we enter a meeting, are likely to be at least provisionally resolved by the time it's over. On one occasion, Jeff's book club spent nearly an hour talking about Mephistopheles's assertion in Goethe's *Faust* that "I am hell itself!" and all the ways that a person can become "hell." Jeff learned a lot from that discussion about Faust and a lot about his fellow book club members! His book club more recently read Stephen Greenblatt's Pulitzer Prize-winning book *The Swerve: How the World Became Modern* about the recovery of Lucretius's ancient manuscript *On the Nature of Things* and how that book then informed the Renaissance and all of modern thought. By the time the evening was over, Jeff had several new interpretations of the title and how the title could inform a deeper understanding of the book.

Michael was swimming in deep water when his club read Lee Smolin's *The Trouble with*

Physics. After participating in his club's discussion, he may not be ready to read a physics journal without some help, but he's grateful to his more scientifically literate book club colleagues for helping him understand the arguments for 5 or 10 or even 26 dimensions. More recently, his club read Lionel Shriver's *We Need to Talk about Kevin* and the women and psychiatrists in the group helped him make sense of the complex psychology of a mother's feeling of alienation and ultimate reconciliation with her mass-murdering son.

As Dewey points out, there's a pleasure in figuring things out. To be sure, one may need to figure something out in order to do a particular kind of work, the focus of our last chapter. But as our stories demonstrate, there's also a pleasure in figuring something out regardless of whether one is immediately going to employ that knowledge. After all, Jeff doesn't plan to become "hell on earth" (and hopes his students would agree that he does not tend in this direction!), nor will he ever be a scholar of ancient or medieval history, and Michael will never be a physicist or, he hopes and prays, the parent of a criminal.

Dewey (1913) labels the pleasure of figuring things out as intellectual pleasure, noting that, "When any one becomes interested in a problem as a problem, and in inquiry and learning for the sake of solving the problem, interest is distinctively intellectual" (p. 83–84). Frijda calls such pleasures aesthetic pleasures, defining them as "disinterested pleasures" or "pleasures resulting from perceiving objects or events without a direct gain or interest being at stake" (p. 83). Our student readers regularly experienced this kind of pleasure (over 250 content units related to intellectual pleasure) and they sought out texts that would provide it to them.

The Pleasure of Solving Problems in General Terms

Our readers talked in general terms about the pleasure they took in the intellectual work they did while reading. Here's Alex in an exchange with Jeff:

JEFF: *So [you like] that puzzle thing, you like having to figure things out?*

ALEX: *I think so, because it's that process of taking the information you have and coming up with possible solutions. Like, it's like being a detective almost. It's taking the evidence and the information and everything that's happened, taking all that and putting it together. Processing through it and seeing what ends connect, and then finding, once all those ends connect, what that last piece is.*

Paul selected readings in order to experience that pleasure. He talked about reading two novels by Alexander Dumas as a sixth grader. When he was asked why, here's how he responded:

> Well, cuz I heard talk about them a lot and I saw that they were really big and I just wanted to take on that challenge and I saw that it had such a big story line, it had so many different ways that you could go through them.

There were so many characters, he had trouble keeping track of them so, "I drew out a family tree of [*The Man in the Iron Mask*]. I think I've still got it sitting around." In response to the question, "So you did that for yourself?" Paul responded, "Yeah, just because I wanted to. I liked the story and I wanted to read it to the best of my abilities." The fact that he's saving that family tree suggests the pleasure and the pride he took in his work.

Paul also discussed that dedication to reading to the best of his abilities with regard to informative texts:

PAUL: *Other ways I play with texts: I will take a text and I will read a sentence, except . . . so say it's the bottom of the page, I'll read that sentence and then I'll move onto the next sentence, kind of going backwards [in ways] that will actually help read the text.*

JEFF: *I see, you read sentence by sentence backwards?*

PAUL: *Yeah.*

JEFF: *Why do you do that?*

PAUL: *Because when you do that you know the end, but you kind of want to know what the beginning is so you're kind of working backwards and you slowly figure out the whole entire puzzle of things and you kind of put it together. It's a pretty good method I've figured out.*

JEFF: *How often do you do that?*

PAUL: *Only for a really, really, long boring text.*

JEFF: *Informational?*

PAUL: *Yeah, informational. Way too informational, like science texts.*

JEFF: *So you make it into a kind of puzzle for yourself?*

PAUL: *Yeah. It's also quite a good way to find quotes from the text, too.*

Of course, not every reader shared Paul's dedication, but we found it striking that the desire for the intellectual pleasure of figuring something out would motivate such a unique and time-consuming strategy.

We also found it striking that the gamers were motivated by a similar pleasure of figuring things out. Here's Robert:

> It's nice to know that I figured it out on my own. Because the philosophy behind the game *Braid* was . . . why not do a game where you actually have to think, have to really work at it, [so] that when they finish it they can feel really good about it. That definitely fits into it, when you can figure something out. Especially when you've been on a puzzle for like a day trying to figure out how to do this one thing. You basically find out what it is you're supposed to do. You feel really good about that.

The Pleasure of Thinking about What Happens Next

Although our informants talked about the pleasure of intellectual work in general terms, they more often focused more specifically on the nature of the intellectual pleasure they experienced. The intellectual pleasure students talked about the most was the pleasure of figuring out what happens next. Helen made that pleasure explicit:

> I like to think also about what the author could have written instead of what they did write, like different endings, like a dramatic part, I'll stop and think about what could happen next, and then read and see what does happen. I just finished reading one, and it's got a really cliffhanger ending, and I haven't bought the next book yet, and I'm coming up with all these ideas about what happened next.

Indeed, one of the pleasures of series books was that they extend the intellectual pleasure of thinking about what plot developments are in store for the reader.

Robert explained that figuring out what happens next is also motivation for game playing:

> Like, in the first *Modern Warfare* there's a part where they drop an atom bomb. You don't see it coming, and it just adds a whole new layer of "there are things going on here that I don't know what will happen next."

Helen was so interested in experiencing the pleasure of figuring out what happens next that she composed her own plots, drawing on the events of the book she was reading:

HELEN: *Sometimes I'll change the character so it's not me or the character really, how it's portrayed in the book. It's just something totally different, I guess, just to make it more dramatic in my own mind. Or if I want the story to go a certain way.*

JEFF: *Wow, this is really interesting because you—it seems to me the stories are not set in stone for you. Like it doesn't have to be the way the author wrote it. That you kind of change the story to meet your satisfaction.*

HELEN: *Yeah, a little bit, like a mad lib. But then I always pull back and read the way the author wrote it.*

Our readers were very mindful of what kinds of texts provided the pleasure of figuring things out. Michelle, for example, took pleasure from stories with a twist. She explained why:

I think that's also why I like twists, like, we live in a crazy world. Anything could happen. And like, just putting twists in there just kind of reminds us to pay attention and try and catch it. It's like a little gold mine to figure out the twists before they happen.

She sought to do similar mining when she played video games:

Yeah. I mean, it's kinda like with video games, but there's different kinds of puzzles I think. I really don't like the logic puzzles in computer games. It's too blunt to me. There's not a side story really, but like there can be twists in a video game in the same way, but it's a whole different platform.

Helen also took pleasure from the unexpected:

I like it when a story does something unexpected. It catches much more of my interest that way. Because sometimes I'll just know how a story is going to end, and I won't even bother to read it. And then I have to go find a new one. So I like the ones where I don't know what's going to happen.

Without some kind of intellectual challenge, there's no reason to read.

Paul concurred:

PAUL: *I used to be into the mystery books and read Sherlock Holmes. I got all the Sherlock Holmes and read them all. And I kind of liked playing the detective and figuring out everything that's happening. But I'm not really much into that anymore because now I can see the plot way too easily in a mystery book whereas other books they'll actually hide the plot a little better than a mystery book sometimes.*

JEFF: *So you want an appropriate challenge and the mystery is not enough.*

PAUL: *Sometimes a mystery can be a challenge, other times not. You just have to pick the right one. So it's just kind of you win some, you lose some.*

Michelle made a similar comment:

Mysteries kind of, the clues are very easy to see once you know the final [outcome]. I mean I've done some Agatha Christie stuff and like she's very, very good at that sort of thing. But you go back, and you're like, "Oh they did that, because of that, and that, and that." And then you just like, it's very obvious. And I mean, if it was a mystery like subplot then that would be very interesting to me. But I feel like if that's the main idea, I like being able to figure things out without being like kind of like, "This is a mystery, now figure it out." Like I can figure out the things that I want to figure out, and if I don't feel like figuring something out then, that doesn't matter because the plot is still going to go on. But that doesn't work in mysteries because if I don't really care anymore about figuring it out then you know, there's no point in reading it anymore.

The Pleasure of Thinking About Characters

Michelle doesn't typically choose texts that provide only the pleasure of figuring out what happens next. Along with the pleasure of figuring out what will happen next, she also sought the pleasure of understanding characters:

I think with a twist comes a character influence or the character is forced to do something they normally wouldn't do. And I think very simple-minded books just don't have that. They don't have the characters, they don't have the realistic aspects of how we can be pushed. Humans can be pushed to do pretty crazy things. Like you hear on the news all the time about people who kill other people, but no one knows the back story to them. So I kind of like to create a little back story to them sometimes.

In contrast, Rori took pleasure in looking forward, in understanding characters' development rather than creating their back stories:

JEFF: *What do you think, what are you most anxious for generally throughout the reading?*

RORI: *I'm most anxious to see the change in the character and how the main character deals with that internally.*

JEFF: *Deals internally with the changes in the situation or the changes in themselves?*

RORI: *Both, just what's happening. That's why I like these books [The Pendragon series] so much because he does it from Bobby's perspective but I like to know what he's thinking and I like to think about what he's thinking and how he's taking the changes that are happening to him.*

Robert was also explicit about the importance of understanding characters:

I think it's very important to me, because I really think if you don't have a good main character, or like, if all the main characters aren't very good at all, I don't think you can really make up for it with like a beautiful background or something like that. I think it's really important to have, especially villains actually. It's important to have a good view on them, especially with villains because you really have to understand why they're doing, why are they the villain? Such as, compared to why is the hero the hero, cuz the hero, they usually provide you with some reason why they do it. They could just be a good person who believes in justice and honor, or they could have a background like Batman or something, like how he had his parents killed so he hates crime. But with the villain, you kind of really have to think why would someone do this. Because it's really annoying when they have the villain and he's just like a mass-murderer who just kills anyone he sees, but they really don't have any reason why. They'll just be like, "Oh, he's mentally unstable," and I'll just be like why? Is it like a genetic thing? Or, is it that he was raised in a situation that ruined his entire mind or something? You really have to build up why would someone do this. And I think it's even more important for the villain, you wonder why they do it as opposed to a hero.

The pleasure of thinking about the characters is what distinguished the books Paul most liked from more exclusively plot-driven narrative such as Choose Your Own Adventure books:

PAUL: *Cuz when you're reading a Douglass Adams book per se you can see satire in a different way. When you're reading a Choose Your Own Adventure it's a flat text that makes you want to go somewhere different. That's what I always thought of it as, flat.*

JEFF: *So Choose Your Own is flat. What do you mean by flat?*

PAUL: *It's flat. You may have different ways to go in a Choose Your Own Adventure book, but with Douglass Adams books you have many different ways you can read it instead of just what page to turn to.*

JEFF: *So what are the different ways you can read it?*

PAUL: *You can read it from a perspective of each of the characters. Like I've read the first book about three times and I've seen it through Marvin, Arthur, and Ford's eyes.*

Choose Your Own Adventure books are flat because they do not provide the intellectual pleasure of taking on the differing perspectives of different characters.

Interestingly, the intellectual pleasure gamers experienced in role-playing games (RPG) stands in contrast to the critique Paul made of Choose Your Own Adventure books. Christian noted that the intellectual challenge of RPG was in creating the characters:

In these games they are RPG and you have to use your imagination and you control your character every step of the way—they don't have the constraints and actions the developer put in. You are in a lot more control. You create and control the character. No map to play on. Your imagination is the map.

The intellectual pleasure our readers took from thinking about and through the characters sometimes motivated their rereading as Paul explained:

JEFF:	*Do you reread a lot of things?*
PAUL:	*Yeah, I do. I like rereading.*
JEFF:	*How is rereading different from the first reading?*
PAUL:	*When you reread it you know the general story line, but then you can look closer about what's happening in the characters' lives and what's happening with the plot, what's happening with the background so you can see it through different angles.*
JEFF:	*So different angles is key for you.*
PAUL:	*I don't know why but it always [is].*

In Chapter 3 we documented the playful pleasures our readers experienced from entering a story world. Quite clearly, our readers also took intellectual pleasure from figuring out those worlds.

The Pleasure of Thinking About Themes

Our readers also took pleasure from abstracting understandings from the texts they read. Callie was especially outspoken about the pleasure she took from making thematic generalizations:

> When I read books, pretty much the plot comes naturally to me and I don't spend a lot of time pondering a plot. [Instead] I kind of ponder myself in the plot. And so, when I read books I do go more philosophical than just feeling the plot and flowing with that and the imagery.

We read this statement as making an explicit distinctions among the playful pleasure of entering a story world ("flowing with that and the imagery"), the pleasure she took from doing inner work ("ponder[ing] myself in the plot"), and a more detached intellectual work.

She expanded this idea later in her interview:

> I think in all reading there are direct and indirect messages you have to look for. I don't know, there are groups that want you to do things their way. Like there are all these metaphors in all these different books I've read that can translate into so many other categories like religion and politics. I think

when you're trying to read a book you read for what you want to find, and if I wanted to find a political message when reading *The Wizard of Oz* I would probably find it, but when I want to find, like, just a story then I'll get that really easily. I think reading about the mob, it could have been a book financed by the mob, written to encourage people but that wasn't what I was looking for. I just kind of enjoyed the book, and when you think about a book after you read it, if you're just reading a book purely for entertainment you'll always have the book in the back of your head. And if you think back like you're trying to figure something out, you'll have that knowledge from the book. You won't have already pulled something from it. Like *Twilight*, I got nothing from that book. But if I think back on that book I could probably pull something from it and use it . . . . So like if there's a book that I've already found something from, like *Cry the Beloved Country*, there's all that tribalism, and so I already have that really zeroed in in my mind of what I want to pull from that book. But like if there's just a book and I read it and I'm like that was just a mediocre book and then I put it down and then I'm thinking about something that related to the topic of the book, then I can think back on that book, and I can pull it in that situation, pull the information, and I can use the information then. Books are just multi-purpose, like you can use them in any way you want. And you can probably use them in a completely different way a few weeks later.

Last chapter we talked about the pleasure of doing inner work through reading. This seems different to us as we see Callie's primary pleasure residing in her ability to do the kind of "pulling" she describes.

Callie took a similar pleasure from rereading her favorite author:

I've reread a few of his [Palahniuk's] books. When I get bored, I just flip to a certain section I like and I reread it. It's nice. I like reading it a lot because any time you read it, you're in a different mood and you can find something different. And you can find something that relates to your life and the world. It's just a nice way to find that freedom in a book, because he is so very free in the way the he writes. It is just wild and wacky and out there in every way.

Once again, the gamers derived a similar pleasure from their game playing. Robert explained that "Video games, they're a way of seeing new ideas." And later "I think it's really, most games kind of have a message to them. Or at least some sort of secondary layer that you can look at." Part of the pleasure of playing them is doing that looking.

The Pleasure of Thinking About an Author's Craft

Our readers also took intellectual pleasure from thinking about the author's craft, a pleasure that motivated rereading for some of them. Here's Helen:

> And when you reread a book you don't have to pay so much attention to the storyline, as much as the little details, you can pick up on those when you've already read it. And I bet if I reread this book right now I'd still find something I didn't catch the first time, even though I've read this like seven times. Some little thing somewhere.

Noticing those little things provided Helen an intellectual pleasure that motivated her rereading.

Earlier we talked about the pleasure our readers took from figuring out what would happen next. Rori explained that her awareness of finding out what happened next could come with the cost of not attending to other aspects of a text. She provided that attention when she reread, as she explained when she talked about *The Soldiers of Halla*, part of the Pendragon series by D. J. McHale:

RORI: *Yeah, cuz a lot happened in between the times that he had been there and you really don't know what has happened because you haven't been there obviously, so it was really confusing and because you like see this desolate place outside that used to be New York and then you see this wonderful place inside the walls and it's just really confusing.*

JEFF: *Does that intrigue you? Is it kind of a mystery?*

RORI: *Yes, it pulls me in. It makes me want to read faster so I can get to what's happening. And sometimes when I do read faster, I skip over all the descriptive stuff, not like purposely but kind of mentally.*

JEFF: *So, you want to get to the plot stuff.*

RORI: *Yeah. Lots of time I'll come back and read descriptive paragraphs like that after I finish the book just to understand what's happening cuz I skim over a lot of that.*

Michelle made a similar comment, though she differs from Rori in that she says her rereading is more pleasurable than her initial reading:

> And I like love rereading books, like everyone makes fun of me because I've read some books at least fifteen times. And like Harry Potter, I've read that so many times. So, I like to see how they made the story happen. Like the first time I read it, it's more like I get really caught up kind of like a reader thing. But like, the more I re-read it I can see, oh, so they put that little information in there so they can like do this really cool twist like four chapters later.

The commentary function in video games lets gamers experience a similar pleasure to the pleasure of rereading, as Robert explained:

> In *Half-Life 2*, I started playing it again and having the thing that you can put the commentary on. That was interesting because you can go around, they have all these speech-bubbly things that come up and you can click on them and you start hearing, "What gave us the idea for this scene was we went down to a meeting and someone suggested it and we said it was hilarious but it wouldn't work and eventually we realized that it actually explained more to do what they said instead of to do something else." In this scene where two people talk, it's actually a glitch where, there's a scene where someone's talking to a robot whose plan to get you across a chasm is to put you in a broken minivan and throw you across, and they have a scene where she says, "You did do the math, right?" And he shakes his head no. That wasn't supposed to happen, but then they decided not to take it out because it was funny and it developed a connection between the characters. It's surprising what you can find out by looking deeper into these games.

Some Textual Conditions that Foster Intellectual Pleasure

Our informants talked about four textual conditions that fostered reading pleasure of the intellectual variety in the context of specific genres.

Fantasy

Helen was articulate about the unique intellectual pleasures readers could take from fantasy, her favorite genre:

HELEN: *Fantasy is written in worlds that don't exist, with things that don't really exist. But it's still about real things most of the*

time, and it often is more than just dungeons and dragons;
it's real life stuff for people who don't like reading about real
life. And it's sort of imagination food. It's like, what if everyone
was still riding horses, and they were also riding dragons? And
there were still knights in shining armor with magical toe rings.
Just, what if? And some people don't get the "What if?" Some
people like the easier what ifs of what if this happened to so-
and-so, in modern day. Other people can't stand that kind of
stuff, and that's what fantasy is for.

JEFF: *What's the good of thinking in these big "What ifs"?*

HELEN: *It gets you out of your own head sort of. It leads to other what*
ifs that could become big ideas that you could follow through
on. It's just fun. [The] "what ifs" game is always fun. Yeah.

Karen shared Helen's enthusiasm for the genre:

I guess I like to read [fantasy] because it kind of explores the unknown and
it's not what you always hear; like if you're watching the news or something
you can hear what's real and the facts but if you're reading fantasy you kind
of get to hear something different. It's a change from what you always see
around us and lots of the time it explores things that have actually happened
just in a different way; some books not all of them, but it's kind of like a
different way to look at it.

Texts They Disagree With

Karen was also an enthusiastic reader of texts with which she disagreed:

KAREN: *I like reading things that I disagree with truthfully because*
it's kind of interesting; it's like I'm totally disagreeing with this
book 100%.

JEFF: *That you're reading now?*

KAREN: *No. It's like well wait why does he want me to believe that and*
maybe I should listen and try to gain the perspective and why
do I disagree with it so much?

JEFF: *Why do you like reading things you disagree with?*

KAREN: *Well it's kind of fun to argue with the book first of all and secondly it's a lot more interesting than reading something you agree with. If you agree with something you're just like "Uh-huh, uh-huh, yeah, yeah," and it's totally what you think it would be, but if you disagree with something you will often take a weird path.*

For Karen, disagreeing promotes more intellectual activity. She has to do more than just say "Yeah, yeah, yeah." And she clearly takes pleasure from that additional intellectual activity.

Visual Texts

We've written before (Wilhelm, 2012c; Smith & Wilhelm, 2006) about how visual texts can be used as a scaffold, arguing that seeing an author's or illustrator's visualizations can help students do their own visualizing. But our research has helped us see these texts in new ways. Here's Rori, a committed reader of graphic novels, in an exchange with Jeff:

JEFF: *Now, are you the kind of reader who looks really hard at the pictures and how they're drawn and what's in there?*

RORI: *The first time I read a book I usually just kind of skim through it and then I'll read it a couple of times and the second time I'll read it, I'll read it for the words and the story, but usually about the third time I read it I'll look at the pictures.*

JEFF: *So you're attending to different things every time through so you're getting different things. Now would you read a fantasy novel in the same way? How is rereading a graphic novel different?*

RORI: *By rereading a graphic novel you have more to look over cuz there's just words in let's say a novel and you can either skim those words or read those words, but in graphic novels you have words and pictures so you can either skim those pictures and get the main idea or you can look at the details and the other things about that.*

Here's how Sharon, our research assistant, responded to Rori's comments in a coding memo:

> She has elevated the graphic novel for me. Previously, I would have said that graphic novels were more of a form for kids who aren't strong readers or who don't like to read. She makes a case for why they are more complex than straight novels and how the visuals can lead to more intellectual work than novels. Hmm.

And Rori wasn't alone in explaining the intellectual pleasure she took from graphic novels. Here's Paul in his think-aloud:

JEFF: *Right, are there any other pictures in here that you really, really like that are worth talking about?*

PAUL: *That was in the beginning. Right here, this picture I thought was interesting because there's a ton going on. Tintin's woken up from a dream and he yells a name and everybody's going crazy and there's champagne glasses and cigarettes and coffee and all sorts of stuff flying. Like there's a little puzzle in the background and I appreciate the scene because it must have taken forever to draw this. It's got a ton of people doing a ton of things. I like a scene in a graphic novel where it will do that, but then you've got to explain it in other panels like right here.*

JEFF: *So do you spend some time kind of looking at it, studying it, going back to it?*

PAUL: *Yeah, like my friends will kind of blow through a comic book or a graphic novel or something and I'll just be going slow and they'll be wondering what's up with me because I like to look at most of the details in the pictures like even in these small panels he has a picture on the wall and he drew the picture very detailed like right there he's got the picture on the wall.*

Once again we learn the lesson that Radway (1984) taught us: You can't understand how texts work unless you understand how readers engage with them.

Pliable Texts

In *Before Reading* (1987), Peter Rabinowitz poses the metaphor of reading as putting together an unassembled swingset. He writes, "It's a concrete thing that, when completed, offers opportunities (more or less restricted depending on the particular swing set involved) for free play, but you have to assemble it first" (p. 38). While he modifies that metaphor in later work (Rabinowitz & Smith, 1998), his essential point remains the same: Authors make texts to be something and readers ought to try to put them together to make that thing. But once they have done so, they have plenty of opportunity for their own constructive work.

Our readers took intellectual pleasure in doing that kind of work. Here's Paul:

> I'll take the book and I'll pick it up, read it and as I begin to read kind of get into a mindset of [seeing] what's going on in the book and I try to see it from different angles. Like I'll see gunshot or something; I'll see a guy jumping and I'll kind of relate it to real life, to pictures I've seen in real life almost and then it's pliable and you can kind of mess around with it.

Paul was not the only reader who took pleasure in that "messing around." So, too, did Helen:

> I change a lot of stories. This book I'm reading right now. . . I just put it down because one of the characters, his friend died and I was really upset cuz I liked that character a lot. And I said, "What if that character didn't die? What if they just got really sick?" and then they had to, I dunno, go get some special root to make them better, and then that didn't work and so a girl was really sad and they thought they were gonna die, and then, miraculously, something happens, and then I can't think of what would happen next. Because I don't want that person to die, but then I go, "Well, they did, and the author must have done it for some reason so I have to find out why the author made that happen." Another thing I change about stories is when I come across a paragraph and I don't like the way the author wrote it, like, the wording is wrong, I'll change the wording in my head, too. "No, they should have switched that around. Independent clause should have come last."

A Word About Intensity, Timing, and Duration

The intellectual pleasure our readers experienced while they read and especially reread was important, though it seems to have been less intense than the pleasures of play and the pleasures of doing inner work, with the noteworthy exception of the readers of graphic novels. We saw fewer exclamations and fewer intensifiers (e.g., really). Perhaps that's because intellectual pleasures were more clearly bounded temporally than the other pleasures. That is, for the most part, they only occurred as the readers were reading. Nonetheless, intellectual pleasure was clearly important to our readers.

WHAT WE CAN LEARN FROM OUR READERS' INTELLECTUAL PLEASURE

Many of the varieties of intellectual pleasures that we document in this chapter seem to us to map onto the typical work of schools pretty closely. After all, we ask students to make predictions, to make inferences about characters, to extract and justify thematic generalizations, and to attend to the author's craft and how this craft works to create meaning and effect. That's very heartening. What's disheartening is that the two readers who were most articulate about the intellectual pleasure they took from their reading were also the most outspoken about how school interferes with that pleasure.

Here's Callie:

> [In out-of-school reading] you don't have the preconceived notion of school. You have "this looks like an interesting book, let's see what it's about." And that just broadens the horizon because without the preconceived notion of what you should be learning, then you don't have the set limits and set expectations for yourself or for the book.

Helen raised a similar concern:

HELEN: *When you pick up a book in school, you know that there's supposed to be something you're getting out of this, and that's all you really think about, what does the teacher want me to understand from reading this. And then, when you read it by yourself, you don't really know what you need to know about it, and it's a little more spontaneous when it happens.*

JEFF: *So, how is that for you, qualitatively? When you are reading something and you learn something that kind of grabbed you, versus going for what the teacher wants?*

HELEN: *Kind of exciting, actually. And fun, like yes, there really is this amazing meaning in this book, and no wonder it's so good. And when you learn something from a book a teacher gives you, it's like, there, now I've found what she was looking for, and now what's the point of finishing this book? And teachers, like, nobody records stuff in the journal when you read the book for* *school. I don't think you think about the book anymore. You're just writing down what you think, and you're thinking about certain things that you think the teacher wants you to think about. When you read a book on your own, you think whatever you want to think. More personal that way, I guess.*

How might we avoid the limitations of which Callie speaks and foster the spontaneity and excitement that Helen finds so compelling? One way would be to read a text for the first time along with our students. Michael and Bill Connolly (Connolly & Smith, 2003; Smith & Connolly, 2005) have written about the benefits Bill experienced from doing just that (though with a focus on poetry).

Another way would be to set up classroom contexts that make it clear that we don't have a specific agenda in mind when we assign reading that we have already done. As we've argued elsewhere (Smith & Wilhelm, 2010), one way to do so is to build units around genuinely debatable questions and to read texts that take different positions on those questions. Still another tactic would be to pair a common reading with some self-selected reading. Imagine asking Rori to compare and contrast the ideas and presentation of one of her graphic novels with a text read in class or Helen to do the same with one of her fantasies or Callie to do the same with an example of dark fiction. Doing so would clearly provide the opportunity, to, in Helen's words, broaden their horizons because it would be impossible to have a preconceived notion of what they should be learning.

Still another idea would be to be mindful of developing patterns of discourse that would manifest that their reading was about more than what the teacher wants. There's a wealth of research that documents how rare open discussions in class are. For example, Applebee, Langer, Nystrand, and Gamoran (2003) found that open discussion of questions that did not have a pre-determined answer averaged only 1.7 minutes per 60 minutes of class time. We've written about this elsewhere (Smith & Wilhelm, 2010; Smith, Wilhelm, & Fredricksen, 2012; Wilhelm, 2007) and very much admire the suggestions about how to foster open discussions made by McCann, Johannessen, Kahn, and Flanagan in their book *Talking in Class* (2006), so we don't want to belabor the point here. But just do a little thought experiment: Think of how different classroom discussions would be if the floor didn't return to the teacher after each student's turn as is the norm, if students got to take five, or six, or even a dozen turns unmediated by the teacher. They would surely be able to take the classroom conversation in whatever direction they wanted it to go.

The good news is that our readers took pleasure from the kind of intellectual activity privileged in schools. The bad news is that school often got in the way of that pleasure.

CHAPTER 6

SOCIAL PLEASURE

"All My Friends Were Telling Me I Had to Read This"

As a young man, Jeff used to visit his high school English teacher Bill Strohm to talk about books. Bill's apartment was lined with bookcases filled with books. After a lively book discussion with Bill, Jeff would invariably leave with a book that he would enthusiastically read so that the next time he saw Bill they could talk about it. Bill probably had more to do with Jeff's becoming an English teacher than any other single person. Jeff learned from Bill, through their book sharing and conversations, that books can transform people and their relationship to the world.

When Jeff was going through high school and college, books were a very important part of his dating strategy. He wanted his girlfriends to understand that he was a reader, and he wanted to be assured that they were readers, too. He often tried impressing his dates with snatches of poetry (when his girlfriend's dog ran away, he quoted Yeats: "Man is in love/and loves what vanishes/but what of that/but what of that/what more is there to say?") or with his talk about particular books, or his love of books in general. Once he found out what kinds of books a girl liked—well, if he liked her enough—he would read one of the books she suggested so that he could talk to her about it. When he was just a high school sophomore, he read Ayn Rand's *The Fountainhead*—a very long book—precisely to impress a senior girl he really liked and wanted to go out with. (FYI: He was successful—at getting the date, anyway!)

As we noted earlier, Michael's dad was a reader. One of the ways they spent time together was to sit on either side of the coffee table in front of the living room picture window reading. They typically sat quietly, each immersed in his book, so when Michael's dad talked, Michael paid special attention. One night when Michael was in eleventh grade, his dad, upon finishing Somerset Maugham's *Of Human Bondage*, exclaimed how much he liked it. The book immediately rose to the top of Michael's queue. Michael was also very taken with the story.

Not long after, Michael stumbled upon Maugham's list of the ten greatest novels ever written: Austen's *Pride and Prejudice*, Balzac's *Pere Goriot*, Brontë's *Wuthering Heights*, Dickens' *David Copperfield*, Dostoevsky's *The Brothers Karamazov*, Fielding's *Tom Jones*, Flaubert's *Madame Bovary*, Melville's *Moby Dick*, Stendahl's *The Red and the Black,* and Tolstoy's *War and Peace*. Michael resolved to read them all. That summer he attempted to do so and did pretty well, though he only made it halfway through *War and Peace,* and *Pere Goriot* was more than he could handle. But by doing that reading, Michael was proclaiming his love for his dad. And, at the same time, he was also establishing himself as the kind of kid who read such books. That summer, Michael worked in an office building and he stood a little straighter when someone in the elevator craned his or her neck to check out the titles of the fat tomes he was carrying.

Our stories suggest the two dimensions of social pleasure that we will be exploring in this chapter: the pleasure of using reading to connect to others and the pleasure of using reading to name and identify yourself. We coded over 300 content units relating to these two dimensions of social pleasure.

THE PLEASURE OF CONNECTING TO OTHERS

Our readers were very clear that part of the pleasure they took from their reading is its social dimension, challenging the cultural image of reading as a solitary activity. Dewey (1913) explains why that image may persist:

> *Adults are so accustomed to making a sharp distinction between their relations to things and to other persons; their pursuits in life are so largely specialized along the line of having to do with things just as things, that it is difficult for them, practically impossible, to realize the extent to which children are concerned with things only as they enter into and affect the concerns of persons, and the extent to which a personal-social interest radiates upon objects and gives them their meaning and worth. (pp. 85–86)*

If Dewey is right (and he usually is, in our view) adults may not fully understand how social interest motivates reading. But our readers certainly did. One obvious way that our readers made a social connection was through their relationships with characters. We've already talked about the pleasure of these relationships throughout this book, but especially in our chapter on the pleasure of play. Dewey (1913), we think, would endorse our choice, as he writes, "A moment's consideration of children's play shows how largely they are sympathetic and dramatic reproductions of social activities" (p. 86). As we've seen, the playful entering of a story world provides similar reproductions. Dewey also notes that "social interest . . . is a strong special interest, and also one which intertwines with those already named" (p. 84). The social interest of connecting with characters intertwines with the pleasure of play; however, the social pleasure of connecting with other readers seems to us to be something different because it happens outside the world of the text.

We were surprised by the length readers went to make their social connections. Here's Mia talking with Jeff about how she became a reader of manga:

MIA: *I read today because it's fun to just find new books and go to the library and like hide in the corner and read, read, read, read. If I don't finish the book I can just take it home. And also, a friend of mine got me interested in manga, and now I go to the library and look for manga. They're like a Japanese comic book, and I like to read Japanese comic books, except for the titles. They're in Japanese.*

JEFF: *Okay, Mia, tell me a little more about manga. You just said that a friend got you interested.*

MIA: *Yeah, a friend of mine. She got a bunch of us hooked on manga, and now she keeps bringing us books and seeing if we like them, because she has a bunch, and she's got me hooked on two things. It's W Juliet and Tokyo Mew Mew. They're just really good. One's an action one and one's a love one.*

JEFF: *How did she get you hooked on these?*

MIA: *She started reading them to us, reading them around us and letting us read them. Teaching us how to read them. Now we go out and buy manga ourselves.*

Mia's friend was so invested in sharing her passion for manga with her friends that she went far beyond simply making recommendations. She read aloud. She taught them how to read the genre. And she shared. Now Mia does the same, at least the sharing. Here she was referring to that same friend:

MIA: *A friend of mine has got a group of us hooked into manga, so I'm reading all of the books that she's read almost.*

JEFF: *And you trade these around with your friends?*

MIA: *Yeah.*

Such extraordinary efforts aren't always rewarded, as Helen explained:

> Nobody I know besides my dad and my brother reads the kind of stuff I do. And I'll find a book I really like, and I'll try to give it to one of my friends and none of them ever likes it. Except my friend Molly does like Tamora Pierce. And we'll discuss that sometimes. And then my friend Emily is like "Shut up! I don't like Tamora Pierce." I physically tried to force her one time to read the books, and she wouldn't do it. Reading it aloud to her, she wouldn't even listen.

But she continued to try:

> I usually, when someone comes over my house, I'll say, "You need to read this book," and I'll let them borrow it. Or make them borrow it.

The notion of forcing someone to read is usually associated with teachers, but our readers so hungered for sharing their books that they did the same. As Sharon pointed out in a memo, the forcing seems motivated differently: "It seems to me the motive is different between these kids and teachers. Teacher coerce more because 'it's good for you;' Helen's forcing is because her pleasure is so intense."

Coercion wasn't always necessary, though. Our readers recognized how powerful books could be and they respected that power when their friends told them about it. Here's Callie:

JEFF: *What do you think drew you to dark fiction in the first place? Do you remember the first book you read?*

CALLIE: *A lot of my friends, they started recommending these books. So I think the first real dark fiction book I read that I started realizing it was dark fiction and that I was into was* Choke. *All my friends were telling me I had to read this . . . . I go to this writing group every Monday and they were telling me this. And*

*I was like sure, and they gave me it and I was like, "Wow, that
was a weird book." So that's how I kind of got into it.*

And as a consequence, she started to do the same: "I've recommended a lot of these
books to people and hope that they will see that in some way and connect with it like
I do."

Recently, her friendship connection through dark fiction took something of a turn:
"Well lately I've been in a competition with one of my friends to see who can finish
all of his [Chuck Palahniuk's] books first, and right now I'm winning." Reading is still
social for Callie, though the nature of how it's social has taken a turn from collaboration
to competition.

Mia made a similar comment about how her friends influence what she reads:

JEFF: *So what are you thinking when you're choosing a book today
that you're going to read?*

MIA: *I usually read the back of the book a little, or occasionally look
to see if I'd understand how to read the book. Also if I read like
the book before I ever get it, and also I usually see if anybody
I knew read the book and if they liked it. If they liked it I would
be more pressured to try it.*

JEFF: *So more wanting to read it?*

MIA: *Yeah.*

JEFF: *Well tell me a bit about that. How is that important?*

MIA: *Because if they liked it I might like it, and then we might both
like the books that are so great.*

JEFF: *So that's important to you to be able to talk about a book with
someone else?*

MIA: *Yeah, because if I could talk about it to someone else, we could
share a view which is really important, because if you don't
know anybody else's view on the book, you don't get a different
meaning or different way of thinking about it.*

What could account for the pressure Mia mentions? Think back to Helen's remarks.
If you love a book, you want those near you to love it as well. And if you do, you can
talk together about it.

Of course, recommendations don't always work out. John didn't like Natalie Babbitt's
Tuck Everlasting, but he read it twice nonetheless:

JEFF: *Tell me some more about why you hate this book.*

JOHN: *I don't know. I read it two times and my sister read it. She called it a great book. I told her no, it's not a good book. It's highly unrealistic. I mean, nobody's ever lived for eternity and lived through a gunshot. I found the story quite entertaining though, how this family is just out in the wilderness, living each day as if it was forever, pretty much, and how everything else is the same as the day before, and on and on.*

JEFF: *If you didn't like it so much, why did you read it two times?*

JOHN: *I read it the second time because my sister [who loved it] made me. She just kept ragging me, like why won't you read it again?*

Why did he acquiesce to his sister's urging? We think it's because he knows how powerfully important books can be and he wants to honor his sister's experience.

Of course, not every social pleasure carries deep meaning. Here's Paul responding to Jeff's question about when he needs to talk about a book:

PAUL: *When it's really deep, when it's got metaphorical stuff that you can talk about, it's got funny parts that you can talk about, it's got stuff that you can relate to the real world, that's when you know you've got a book that you need somebody to talk to.*

JEFF: *That's really interesting, that's come up a few times when talking about the idea that humor needs to be shared.*

PAUL: *Yeah, it does. That's kind of how humor goes.*

JEFF: *I like that; it's kind of how it goes.*

PAUL: *Yeah, so I mean, if you've got a hilarious joke you're not going to want to sit there remembering it to yourself you're kind of gonna want to pass it on. It's kind of like that with books, too. Or when it's really hilarious I'll like find somebody who knows about these kinds of books and I'll show them a funny part of the book because it's so funny.*

As we saw last chapter, books can provide the opportunity to do important work, and talking with others helps do that work, but other things, like humor, may not be so portentous; nonetheless, they demand sharing—that's kind of how it goes.

The deeper stuff plays a particularly important role in developing relationships. Here's Karen talking about her friendship circle:

> We've all been friends since kindergarten. We kind of grew up as readers. It kind of, it has spurred a lot of conversation; maybe some deeper thought. It has shaped some things in our friendship.

We've experienced the same kind of deepening in our book clubs. The books we've read over the years with our book club colleagues have spurred conversation about the most important issues and ideas we face in this world, a kind of conversation that one only has with one's most intimate friends.

Sharing also enhanced the intellectual pleasure of figuring things out. Here's Robert:

ROBERT: *A lot of my friends are also into science fiction, they're nerds kind of. We try and find out more about what goes, we like to, but we also try to find out what goes around in our world and try to compare what goes on within it. Like my friend, he read* The Giver, *and it's pretty much future communism. And I've heard about how* The Giver *pretty much is that, kind of. Or you hear, like, we say* The Matrix *is similar to pretty much Buddhism and the idea that our world is just an illusion, cuz the figure in that is a moral delusion because you can only get pain from an illusion. We try and compare things within the science fiction to real things, just simplify it out and smooth it out and explain like what the whole idea behind it is.*

JEFF: *When you do this, do you just hang out?*

ROBERT: *Yeah, it's usually when we're just hanging out. We really like to talk about books and movies and games and stuff that we're into.*

JEFF: *So is that part of the joy of reading, that you can share and talk about these things with your friends?*

ROBERT: *Yeah. It's kind of a book club that has no actual meetings in a way. We just kind of whenever we see each other we'll just talk about it.*

Interestingly, the gamers among our readers experienced the same kind of social pleasure through their games. John explained the social pleasure associated with multiple player games. "Yeah, they just appeal to me, as it's fun in one respect, but also . . . you're playing with other people online, and it's like a force, you have to work together. It's just a feeling."

Our readers not only used their reading to derive social pleasure connecting with their friends, they also used reading to derive social pleasure from their relationship with their families. In fact, Paul's reading was initially motivated by a family connection as he poignantly explained: "In sixth grade my grandmom died and she was the one who really taught me how to read, and it was kind of almost a spark and I started reading a lot." Just as Michael was connecting with his dad as he struggled through Maugham's reading list, Paul was connecting with his grandmom whenever he read.

Paul also made it clear that his family connections through reading go beyond his grandmom and are not all so poignant:

> My parents, my mom reads everything and my dad reads really good novels. And so both of them kind of like the sci-fi things and my mom really likes the Terry Pratchett books, she'll steal them from me. I got the newest one and instantly it was magically gone from my room.

Far from being annoyed with the disappearance, he embraces the connection.

Helen also talked about making a family connection through reading in a quote that Sharon labeled as one of her favorites in the whole data set. In it she talked about going book shopping with her dad:

> When I take [the books] home, actually, I start reading my book on the car ride back from the book store most of the time. My dad and I always go to Baja Fresh after the book store, because it's right there and pretty good Mexican food. We have an inside joke, we say, "Are we going to eat like people or are we going to read and eat at the same time," and I say, "Dad, shush I'm reading."

"I love her dad," Sharon wrote in a memo. It's quite obvious that Helen does, too.

The Pleasure of Naming Yourself

We depart from Dewey's formulation in the second section of this chapter, for he saw social interest solely in terms of one's engagement with others. Psychologist Erik Erikson (1963) justifies this departure by arguing that the central psychosocial conflict of adolescence is identity versus role confusion. That is, adolescents have to make a place for themselves in the social worlds they inhabit. Doing so, he claims, depends on a confidence in one's sameness and continuity that's matched by a sameness and continuity in one's meaning for others. Identity work, according to Erikson, has a social dimension.

In recent years the notion of a stable identity has been challenged on a variety of fronts. Sharon has been our guide through the murky waters of identity theory. She's identified three different positions theorists take on identity:

- identity as taxonomic (individuals have multiple identities that perform differently in different contexts)
- identity as hierarchic (although individuals may have multiple identities, some are closer to the core than others)
- identity as hybridized (individuals can perform multiple identities simultaneously in particular contexts, creating new hybrid combinations)

We don't want to engage in this debate now, for our data make it clear that whether identity is singular or multiple, performed or inherent, a number of our readers used their reading to name themselves and to differentiate themselves from others. We see this as different from the kind of inner work we explored in Chapter 4. Inner work is designed to develop self-awareness. Naming oneself is designed to articulate one's place in the world and is therefor a kind of social effort and pleasure.

Rebecca did this naming most clearly:

> When I meet somebody and I'm holding a book, they're like, "Oh, you like books?" I'm like "Yeah, I'm totally a bookworm." That's what I say. Everybody in my family is a bookworm so I'm a bookworm. That's how I identify myself.

John's identity is more complex (or more clearly multiple), yet reading is a crucial component, for, as we have seen, it's reading that has allowed him to learn and to see multiple perspectives:

JOHN: *Most important things [about me]: I have to travel, I have to be able to learn other things, I have to see things in different perspectives, I have to play gaming at least 12 hours a week and during summer at least 24 hours a week. And I have to know my facts before I actually try to debate them, unlike some of my classmates. They can go out and connect facts together that don't even make sense. That creates conflict even more.*

JEFF: *Okay, now tell me how your reading fits in with these essential things about being John.*

JOHN: *Well, I recently played on a soccer team with high school students and they were talking about what textbooks* *they were reading. I was like, "Why don't you actually read some good books? And they were like, "I basically just read textbooks for school." They never found the joy of reading. And they were pretty smart, [but] they just only read books for school and requirements. They never read for fun. But out of that they just want to know what they need to know. They basically got to the line of what they had to get to and stopped at that. I go to the line and I continue and look at different facts. I don't look at the past that much. I mean, I don't read history too much to actually see the past as today, but I know what can change the outcome of today and how we learn from it.*

Robert embraces the identity of a nerd. And his reading is an important part of that embrace:

That's hard to explain. Geekism is when you focus on one thing and involve that significantly into your life. Basically, geek is just used as a derogatory term. Like computer geeks, just because [they] seemed weird at the time. Now it's usually seen as, I focused on this one thing in my life. Nerdism though is basically a lot of the geekisms put together. Usually, if you're interested in video games, books, certain movies, certain genres, all kind of at the same time then you're basically a nerd. And you can be a geek while being a nerd at the same time, because you can be a nerd and have one specific part of the nerd culture that you focus on and that makes you a geek of that.

The readers we have discussed thus far thought of their reading as an important identity marker and talked about reading in general terms. In contrast, when Callie talks about who she is, she named herself not as a reader in general terms, but rather as a reader of dark fiction:

I'm really passionate about whatever I want to be doing, no matter what it is. I'm not easily discouraged at all. I love acting. I'm really energetic. I'm really weird. I don't know how else to describe it, but I'm weird in the way that I'm not self-conscious, I'm weird in the way that there aren't inhibitions like most people. I can read dark fiction and not be disturbed by it. . . and everyone can give me a weird look like she's crazy and I really won't care. I'm just weird.

And again:

> I think because a lot of the things about me is I'm honest with who I am, and the books I read are blatantly honest, whether it's about the characters or the culture or whatever's happening. They don't cover it up with sugary euphemisms. They actually say it. And they make it so much easier to relate to and to understand. Like *Choke*, it's not like, "Oh my grandma's really sick, oh I'm really worried." No. His grandma's dying, and he has to drop out of med school to support her. It doesn't sugarcoat things, and I don't sugarcoat things. As sweet and energetic as I am, I am honest about who I am and who I'm gonna be and I like my reading the same way. I don't like to have a heroine that's blonde and blue-eyed and perfect in every way. She's skinny and tall and pretty and everyone loves her! That's completely fake. I think because I am okay with who I am and I'm honest about who I am it's hard for me to read it when people aren't.

Interestingly not all of our readers were willing to grant the connection between reading and identity. Here's Helen:

> No. I notice that some people have that kind of thing, like "I'm a fantasy reader, ooh that makes me different, which means I'm myself." That's something I really hate, when people think just because they're making a point to be different they're being themselves. Sometimes yourself isn't all that different. Then it's just obnoxious, and that's just their excuse to be annoying. "It's me, I don't want to change. Ooh." You're just being obnoxious. You want people to squirm at your high-pitched voice.

And later:

> No, no, . . . the people who read the manga stuff, their life becomes centered around their genre, and they never branch out of it and they only hang out with people, I noticed, who only read manga stuff. It just seems like there should be more to it than that, than just something to revolve around, somewhere to put yourself, I think it is just a way to classify yourself. "I'm a comic book reader; I'm a divergent thinker because I read comic books." No, you just read comic books. That should be it.

In like manner, our participants differed in the extent to which they saw their gaming as an identity marker. Wesley didn't embrace his nerdiness with quite the same enthusiasm that Robert does, but ultimately he does embrace it:

JEFF: *Now what does it mean to be a nerd?*

WESLEY: *A nerd, like, always playing video games, really technologically geeky and stuff.*

JEFF: *Do you think that applies to you?*

WESLEY: *I am kind of a nerd. I am technologically savvy, and I know what to do.*

JEFF: *So it's not necessarily a critique or a bad thing.*

WESLEY: *No. I don't see it as a critique; I kind of see it as a compliment if someone calls me a nerd. But other people want to call you a nerd because they think it will get you down. But ultimately it doesn't for me.*

In contrast, despite Jeff's urging, Terry echoed Helen in not accepting that his playing a particular game said anything about him:

JEFF: *So if I said, "Terry loves Assassin's Creed," what would you think?*

TERRY: *I would just think that he likes a good game, and he has a good choice in gaming. I mean, there's not a whole lot that carries over. Maybe I could say that he has an interest in ancient architecture and things like that.*

JEFF: *Would you say that? Like, let's say you didn't know Terry. I just said I have a guy and he loves Assassin's Creed, and I said what do you think about that? What would you say?*

TERRY: *A LAIR player. That's what I would say.*

JEFF: *A layer player?*

TERRY: *A LAIR is, like, live action intense role-playing. And you have foam swords and you play on a battlefield and attack each other. Kind of strange. . . .*

JEFF: *Is there anything else you would expect about this guy who likes Assassin's Creed?*

TERRY:	*Not really. I mean, you can't tell just by the game.*
JEFF:	*So now this is what I'm hearing you say, Terry, so correct me if I'm wrong, is that if a guy likes a game [it] really doesn't mean anything to you about his life. There's nothing you can really predict.*
TERRY:	*No, not really. Everybody plays different games. It doesn't really make them who they are.*

Our readers differed on the extent to which their reading was an identity marker. But it clearly was for some. They were unanimous in taking pleasure from the social dimension of their reading, however.

A Word About Intensity, Timing, and Duration

Social pleasure, in our view, worked differently for our readers than did the other kinds of pleasures. When our readers talked about the pleasures of play, work, and figuring things out, they tended to talk about discrete events, the reading of a particular book, for example. In contrast, the social pleasures they discussed provided the context in which these other pleasures were embedded (their connection with friends and family) or were the culmination of those pleasures (naming themselves as readers). In both cases, social pleasures were both intense and enduring.

What We Can Learn From Our Readers' Social Pleasure

As you've seen throughout the book thus far, our readers weren't reluctant to say what teachers shouldn't do. However, they seldom talked about what teachers should do. That's why their enthusiasm for peer discussion was so striking. Here's Callie talking about discussions both with her peers and her teacher:

JEFF:	*So how could teachers make sure or encourage kids to get the most out of reading?*
CALLIE:	*I think talking about it. Like we have a lot of class book discussions, and those are all like exactly the education value you want to get out of it, and we have to discuss that. I think having kids discuss with each other and with the teacher what books they're reading and have the teacher not judge them*

about it. I know [my teacher] reads some good books and
books I like, too, and so we've had some good discussions
about these books and it makes me think about these books
and enjoy these books more. I think a lot of teachers wouldn't
really understand that.

What's especially noteworthy here, we think, is Callie's recognition of her teacher as a fellow reader, not just an authority. We argued earlier that reading a text for the first time along with our students is a practice that can foster authentic conversations. Callie would agree.

Rori focused on small group discussions:

One of my favorite books was probably *The Power of One* by Brice Courtenay. I loved reading that in class cuz it was a class book and I loved discussing it with my peers cuz we were assigned to book groups. There were four in my group. That was a really good reading experience for me cuz I could also see how my peers visualized it. And what they got out of it metaphorically.

Rori makes it clear that she loves small-group discussion when she and her peers have a chance to talk about important issues. We suspect she'd feel far less strongly about what Nystrand (1997) calls collaborative seatwork, in which students work together to fill out single answer worksheets and the like. He distinguishes such seatwork from authentic conversation-like small group discussions and finds that it has a negative effect on student learning.

Authentic conversations, on the other hand, are those that allow for real exploration, as in the pair work that Paul so enjoyed:

JEFF: *Were there other things the teacher did that made it work for you?*

PAUL: *Well we'd have to share it with a partner.*

JEFF: *Was that good?*

PAUL: *Yeah that was good because we could see our angles from reading the thing and see "Oh wow they've got a completely different, that's another way to look at it" and then we'd go to another group and there would be tons of different ways to look at it. And it's like, yeah, that's cool.*

JEFF: *So, there's this thing going on here about multiple perspectives that you like—you like being shocked into seeing things in a new way.*

PAUL: *Yeah, because I don't like it when you've just got your own opinion and you're like "okay, that's my opinion." But what do other people think about it and then you can build these other people and see from their eyes and see from your eyes and see from another person's eyes and then see from another person's eyes and build these multiple angles [from] which to look at it.*

Once again, it's crucially important that the "it" to which Paul refers in his final turn is an idea or text sufficiently complex to allow for multiple perspectives.

In short, then, our readers suggested that teachers work to encourage conversation-like discussions in which they can be participants. Reading texts for the first time along with our students is also a way to foster the social pleasure of connecting with others, as Michael and Bill Connolly (Connolly & Smith, 2003) found out. Here's what one of Bill's students wrote about his writing in his response journal when Bill read along with the class:

> Whatever came to mind, I wrote. There was nothing holding me back. The teacher had not read the poem before, so he was doing the same thing as me—trying to understand it.

And here's what Bill wrote in his teaching journal about participating in classroom discussions in such a situation:

> I like how I felt comfortable not knowing it all and equally comfortable giving my opinion or interpretation.

And later:

> I have to say that I feel there was respect for my authority (as teacher) but a number of kids had no qualms about disagreeing with me. . . . I feel good about that type of authority. My kids feel comfortable disagreeing with me.

Another implication seems to us to be to devise classroom contexts in which students can recommend reading to others. Maybe some kind of classroom Goodreads site would do the trick. Classroom book clubs would as well. There are many book-length treatments of this topic, so we won't explore specific suggestions here except to share the unique approach our friend Steve Littell took with his middle-schoolers. Steve wanted to maximize the social pleasures of the clubs, so he set them up just the way his book club worked. Each meeting a different student was the host. The host chose the book, got the conversation started with some kind of question or comment, and brought treats to share. After the discussion, book club members simply wrote a quick summary of the issue that began the conversation and rated the treats that were brought in.

Our readers did not make any explicit suggestions for how teachers could foster the social pleasure of naming oneself, and, as we noted, that pleasure is not one that all of our readers experienced. But if they are to do so, it's obviously important that they have plenty of opportunity for choice. It's hard to name yourself through reading texts someone else has chosen.

If you Google *Hotel Lobby* by Edward Hopper you'll see the image of a solitary woman reader. But our readers paint a different picture. They invite us to consider a prequel to the picture. Imagine a close friend telling the woman that she has a book the woman just has to read. Now imagine a sequel in which the two of them talk excitedly about the book they now share in common. Our data on social pleasures also led us to wonder why the woman went down to the lobby to read instead of staying in her room. Might it have been to announce to the world that she was a reader? There are social pleasures to reading. We have to make sure we give our students a chance to experience them.

CHAPTER 7

READERS OF THE HEART

Getting Carried Away by Romances

Thus far we've talked about the nature and variety of pleasure our participants experienced in their reading. While we mentioned particular books and genres, we didn't spotlight them. We'll be paying that kind of focused attention now in Part 2 of the book. As noted when we explained our method, we interviewed another group of informants, slightly older adolescents than the eighth graders whose responses we featured in the first half of the book, who were deeply committed readers of a particular genre. Jeff also visited with interest/friendship groups that were organized around reading the specific genres, groups to which the case study informants usually belonged. Additional data came from Jeff's teaching: his classroom journal and observations, surveys, and assessments he did over the years.

Our case study informants experienced a range of reading pleasures in different ways across specific genres. However, as our informants explained, the pleasure of inner work associated with reading was profound for all in the playful, intellectual, or social pleasures they enjoyed. We've already introduced the notion of inner work in our chapter on work pleasure. However, because we found that our case study readers tended to be committed to a particular genre because of the inner work that genre allowed them to do, we'll begin this chapter with a more extended exploration of a few aspects of depth psychology before turning to our discussion of romance, the first genre we'll consider.

Depth Psychology

By depth psychology we mean, like Clifford Mayes (2007), "any view of the psyche that takes seriously the idea that *personal subconscious processes* and *collective unconscious processes* affect how one consciously experiences and acts in the world" (p. 11). The work of depth psychology was born in the seminal work of Freud and particularly Carl Jung, and has been significantly developed in the more recent work of D. W. Winnicott, W. R. D. Fairbairn, Heinz Kohut, and many others.

Depth psychology maintains that the goal of life is to achieve psychological wholeness and a deep relationship to oneself, others, the environment, and the Self—capitalized to denote the transpersonal elements of one's personhood. Depth psychologists recognize the importance of personal psychology and personal issues such as identity, power, and sexuality, but they go beyond these to also focus on higher functions that involve relationships with others, society, the environment, and what might be called the sacred or divine.

Inner Work and Depth Psychology

As we explained in Chapter 4, inner work can be defined as any effort taken to communicate with and integrate one's unconscious, repressed, or unlived potential into conscious mindfulness and life. According to depth psychology, the unconscious communicates through imagination, art, feelings, dreams, stories and symbols. Jung claimed that 98% of all mental activity is irrational and from the unconscious, and that modern western culture ignores the unconscious to its great loss and peril. Jung's studies of native peoples around the globe, such as the Navajo and Australian aboriginals, led him to claim that native peoples spend upwards of 70% of their time dealing with the unconscious through dream interpretation, storytelling, and ritual. Indeed, in those cultures, daily activities such as cleaning, food gathering, and the preparation of meals are ritualized in highly symbolic ways. Jung maintained that the psychic health of people and communities who have maintained traditional lifestyles was very high.

Current evolutionary psychology, cognitive psychology, and neuroscience all support the contentions of depth psychologists regarding the extent, role, and influence of the unconscious (sometimes referred to as the automatic and affective systems) as well as the healthful effects of inner work such as meditation, cognitive therapy, dream interpretation, and the like (Haidt, 2006). Research demonstrates that relating to the unconscious is important to the development over time of nuanced feeling and aesthetic experience, which in turn are essential to human evolution (Dissanayake, 1992). Contemporary neuroscience and psychology has likewise shown inner work to be essential to the development of individual moral life (Damasio, 2005). (For excellent reviews, see Damasio, 2010; Haidt, 2006).

The goal of life, according to depth psychology, is to individuate, or to become one's most whole and fully integrated self. According to Goldbrunner (1965), individuation means becoming "an individual being, in so far as we understand by individuality our innermost, ultimate, and incomparable uniqueness" (p. 94). The enlightened consciousness of the individuated self, according to Jung, involves both understanding one's complete self more consciously and understanding one's connection to others, the world, and some sense of the animating spirit of the universe—what most of us would call the divine. We believe that this very process was undertaken by our case study readers as they read and responded to their reading.

Archetypal Patterns

Jung and his followers have focused more than any other depth psychologists on the role of myth and archetypes in human psychology, so one way we'll examine our informants' engagement with, and response to, specific genres is through an archetypal lens. According to Jung, an archetype is a primordial, structural element of the human psyche. Jung defined an archetype as a universal pattern, motif, or insight that comes from the collective unconscious, the place where individual "human consciousness and transcendent consciousness intersect" (Mayes, 2010, p. 29).

In his studies of the underlying structure of the human personality, Jung paid special attention to myths and to mythological figures across time and culture, and examined how these were expressed in individual dreams and imaginative activity.

Jungians argue that myths and cultural stories are a special kind of literature produced not by an individual but by an entire age and culture. We might regard these stories as the distillation of the needs, dreams, and expressions of an entire culture or of humanity as a whole. These stories seem to evolve slowly over time as certain motifs emerge, are elaborated, and as people tell and retell the stories and retain only those elements that catch and hold their interest and speak powerfully to them over time. In this way, the themes that are informative and universal are kept alive, while those that are particular to subgroups or to an era drop away.

Myths, therefore, are true in that they express a deep and universal human pattern, depicting levels of reality that go beyond our rational way of thinking about the external world and that extend our receptivity to and even our thinking about the inner world. Modern man's ignorance of the mythic truths of the inner world is reminiscent of Hamlet's injunction that "There are more things in heaven and earth, Horatio, than are dreamt of in your philosophy!"

WHY ROMANCE?

We start with romance because of all of the genres we'll be considering, it's the one about which we had the most concerns. We're both fathers of two daughters and from the time they were infants we were wary of what books (and other cultural texts) might teach them about how to be a woman in the world. A decade or more after the fact, we discovered that both of us banished Shel Silverstein's *The Giving Tree* from our daughters' bookshelves because it tells the story of the sacrifices the female tree makes for a decidedly unworthy man. We resisted reading *Cinderella* as best we could (Disney is a formidable foe!) because it chronicles the rescue of a strong woman by a handsome prince. The concerns we felt for our daughters extended to our female students. Remember our discussion of Michael's worry about the Sweet Valley High books many of his female students were reading?

We're not alone. Some critics critique the romance novel's lack of suspense, and question whether it is healthy "for women to be whiling away so many hours reading impossibly glamorized love stories" (Gray, 2000, p. 3). But Gray complicates this stigma, by arguing that it might be rooted in sexism because romance is the only genre "written almost exclusively by women for women" (p. 3).

To learn about the pleasure committed readers of romance experience, Jeff talked at length with Kylie, a deeply dedicated reader of romances. Kylie is a very articulate girl who excels in English and wanted to major in English in college, with the goal of becoming a YA author or romance writer. Kylie went underground about her romance reading habit through middle school and most of high school, though she now acknowledges it. She's always been open about her passion for romance with family and select friends. Those friends shared romances and their responses to what they were reading, which often included ranking books, writing fanfics that transformed the original stories, seeing and critiquing romantic comedies, and other associated activities. During the time of the study, her friendship circle passed around John Green novels and discussed these both in-person and online.

The Romance Writers of America association cites two criteria for a story to qualify as a romance: 1) it must focus on the development of a romantic relationship, and

2) it must have a happy ending. That simple formula has been enormously successful. According to The Romance Writers of America website, sales of romances topped a billion dollars in 2010, far outperforming any other genre despite the stigma that romances face.

The genre has a long history. The famed Jungian analyst Robert Johnson (1983) cites *Tristan and Iseult,* composed in the 12th century, as the first modern romance. He argues that the romance appeared exclusively in western culture because the material progress of Europe required separating functional work from ritual, the real from the sacred, the everyday from the idealized, the rational from the irrational. But, he argues further, this separation has caused many wounds.

Romances, he contends, can be a way to examine or even to heal those wounds and to re-integrate parts of our whole being that have been traditionally separated, or to bring back into consciousness qualities that we have repressed. To do so is to move towards the goal of wholeness, of consciously embracing and accepting our entire being.

Johnson's analysis of *Tristan and Iseult* illustrates the power of romance in encouraging that movement. In the story, Tristan escorts Iseult the Fair to her appointed wedding with his liege, King Mark. It is a hot day and they mistakenly drink the love potion meant for the bride and groom and fall helplessly in love. Many adventures ensue during which their affair is consummated, Iseult the Fair violating her wedding vows and Tristan his fealty to his uncle and king. Their relationship, so intense and passionate, is a hopeless disaster for themselves and everyone around them. Eventually, Tristan finds himself in France, where he helps to save a kingdom from evil enemies. The French king offers Tristan his daughter, Iseult of the White Hands, as a bride. They marry but Tristan, reminded by a token of Iseult the Fair, cannot consummate the union and all falls apart.

It's no mistake that both women are named Iseult. Iseult the Fair is the archetypal ideal woman. She is sacred and unattainable. Iseult of the White Hands is a real woman, who knits and cooks with her hands. Tristan's true tragedy is that he foregoes the love of a real woman and the joys of a real relationship because he is in thrall to an unattainable idealized notion of womanhood and relationship. (Not that this happens today!) We will see in a bit how this tension between the ideal versus real played out in Kylie's reading.

Johnson explains that this legend appeared as a warning at the moment in history that westerners began to worship the ideal archetypal woman through the cult of chivalry. The legend teaches us that if we confuse the archetypal and ideal with the real, we will come, like Tristan and Iseult, to ruin. Consciously understanding the transpersonal archetypal values of womanhood, love, integration, and the like is important, but even more so is creating personal images and values that can be lived out in healthy ways in the real world.

Romance stories have continued to be significant in western culture across time. Samuel Richardson's famed *Pamela, or Virtue Rewarded* (1740), was the first successful romance novel in English—indeed one of the earliest novels—and was a breakthrough on at least two other counts—it was told from a female perspective as an epistolary novel, and it focused almost entirely on relationship and courtship. This focus on the feminine and on female readership continues to this day.

Jane Austen further developed the genre; *Pride and Prejudice* (1813) is considered a classic romance. Inspired by Austen, Georgette Heyer introduced historical romances, specifically the Regency romances, with the publication of *The Black Moth* in 1921. In the thirties, due in part to the huge success of Heyer, the British company Boon and Mills began releasing lines of what are known as "category romances," short formula-driven books, often in serial form, meant to be consumed quickly. These books were licensed for sale in North America to Harlequin Enterprises, which began direct marketing to readers and allowing mass-market merchandisers to carry the books.

In the United States, the single-title modern romance genre exploded on the scene in 1972 with Avon's publication of Kathleen Woodiwiss's *The Flame and the Flower*. Romance sales boomed in the 1980s, with the addition of many category romance lines and an increased number of single-title romances. Popular authors began pushing the boundaries of the genre and plots, and characters began to explore modern dilemmas.

As we'll see, these modern romances (at least the ones read by our participants) speak to deeply felt needs. Kylie made that abundantly clear in her definition of a "real" romance. Kylie's first experience with romance novels were from the Twilight series, but as a more experienced reader of romances she critiqued those novels as shallow because the main characters just fall in love:

They don't go through a long challenge of really getting to know each other. [The Twilight books] are more about infatuation or attraction than real love. It's okay to start out like that but there is no development and that is necessary.

She continued:

Now I am really against the Twilightification of romance—a young kind of love where you just are in love and it just happened, it didn't develop, not a real experience that was deeply felt and developed. . . . [The way the couple] comes to treat and see each other has to be unconventional and unique and special and recognize something about [each] person's uniqueness. I want someone to do that for me and that kind of thing is never easy. It really bothers me when there are romance stories like *Twilight* where she falls in love with him just because he's strong or powerful or saves her or whatever.

> That can be the start but that is not the thing. Where people don't see the depth in each other and struggle to get beyond the surface, I'm just like GAH, that's not a real romance . . . . [A real romance] is where people really work and eventually come to recognize the reality of each other. . . . Then there can be real long-term happiness.

The focus of Kylie's critique echoes Jung's notion of simple immersive consciousness, a state that's highly attractive as it requires no struggle or pain but one that must be outgrown if people (or characters) are to be able to enter complex and then enlightened states of consciousness and relationship.

Kylie's definition of a real romance uncannily mirrors not only the injunction to differentiate the common archetypal structure and the personal archetypal image, but also mirrors the interpretations depth psychologists give to the archetypal story of Psyche and Eros. We think that mirroring is so interesting that it's worth a close look at the myth and how it signifies.

Before we take that close look, it's important to note that Jungians and like-minded depth psychologists see the world as being divided into masculine and feminine energies. Likewise, they see each individual as also divided into masculine and feminine energies. While a male, in such a view, is dominated by his masculine energy, he possesses feminine energy as well, which Jung called the *anima*. Females, in turn, possess male energy, which Jung called the *animus*. Jung defined the anima as the inner feminine side of man, as well as the archetypal image of womanhood in a man's psyche. The anima is also the conduit to communication with the unconscious. In Jungian interpretations of the myth of Psyche and Eros, therefore, the figure of Eros represents masculinity, whether it is found in man or woman, whereas Psyche represents femininity wherever it is found. (Note: Our archetypal interpretations of this myth are embedded in parentheses.)

The myth relates that Eros falls in love with the mortal but charismatic Psyche, much to the dismay of his mother, Aphrodite. Aphrodite had sent Eros to make Psyche fall in love with and marry a monster as punishment for taking the attention of humans away from the cult of Aphrodite. In undertaking this task, Eros pricks himself with one of his own arrows and falls in love with the vision of Psyche (simple immersive pleasure and simple consciousness/infatuation). He marries her himself and takes her to a valley of paradise, but he will only come to her in darkness so she will not recognize him. He forbids her to look on him or ask him about himself (the desire to stay infatuated and in simple consciousness). Psyche's sisters insist that Eros must be the monster that was promised her by the jealous Aphrodite and declare that she should shine a light on him as he sleeps and then kill him. Psyche lights the lamp, sees Eros, and falls even more deeply in love with him. Oil from the lamp awakens Eros, who flees and leaves Psyche utterly and completely alone (signaling the entrance into complex consciousness and the true challenges of a relationship). She wanders the world trying to reclaim Eros, and after supplicating every god and goddess in the Pantheon, all of whom reject her, she becomes the slave of Aphrodite (indicating that we must go to the source of the problem, and Aphrodite is the goddess and archetype of romantic love).

Aphrodite sets Psyche on four seemingly impossible tasks (such challenges must always be overcome to achieve enlightened consciousness). First she is made to sort millions of seeds. Though Psyche despairs, she is helped by ants to achieve the goal (the ants representing the archetypal feminine ordering/organizing principle). She then gathers wool from the violent rams of the Sun, not by shearing them, but by gathering the wool they have left on briars and branches (the archetype of subtle indirect feminine power, and of taking only what is needed instead of being greedy and exploitive). Then Psyche is helped to procure a goblet of water from the middle of the River Styx by an eagle (an archetype of feminine far-sightedness, of seeing the big picture). Finally, Psyche is made to go to Hades and bring back the beauty of Persephone and Death in a casket. But she opens the casket before reaching the light and falls unconscious, and Eros, touched by her feminine dedication and energy, disobeys his mother and saves Psyche (achieving reciprocity, a necessary element of relatedness, and leading to the integration of masculine and feminine elements). They are married on Olympus and she becomes immortal (constituting the achievement of wholeness and enlightened consciousness).

Although this story is primarily about the feminine and about relationship, it is important to note that Eros, the male in the story, does come to appreciate the real feminine virtues of Psyche and rebuffs his mother, who symbolizes the idealized archetype of romantic love. When he does so, Psyche and Eros are integrated into a whole.

The Jungian archetypal interpretation of this myth is quite complex (we have provided a very simplified version), but for now suffice it to say that Psyche and Eros move from being "in love," an inflated and short-term paradise-like state of unconscious infatuation, through many struggles and challenges of getting to know and love each other, to loving each other's true selves and appreciating each other's true personhoods. In Jungian terms, they have moved from simple consciousness to complex consciousness to enlightened consciousness (an integration of understanding the reality of both the external world and the inner world).

Robert Johnson (1989) provides an illuminating quotidian gloss on these stages of consciousness when he says that in simple consciousness we walk home and wonder enthusiastically what is for lunch; in complex consciousness we walk home and wonder about fate and the imponderables of the universe, worrying all the while about our individual lives; and in enlightened consciousness we have struggled with the imponderables until we have integrated our inner world with the external world to the point that we now again enthusiastically wonder what is for lunch, living fully and consciously by embracing the wonders and potential of each moment. A real romance, according to Kylie, takes its characters through all three stages.

The Pleasures Readers Get From Reading Real Romances

Kylie, our primary informant, and her friends, who were also romance readers, took great pleasure in their engagement in these real romances.

The Pleasure of Play

The avid readers of romance to whom we spoke were articulate about the pleasure they took from giving themselves over to the story. Kylie had this to say:

> My favorite part [of romance] is before they know—when they don't like each other yet, or are attracted but are overcoming problems, or maybe are just starting to discover how to love each other.

She continually referred to the steps in this process as "cutesy" and "thrilling." In discussing John Green's YA romance *An Abundance of Katherines*, Kylie asserted that:

> What was satisfying in his [Colin's] relationship with the new girl, [was that] he became more fully himself, more active, more dominant, and he realizes this new personal growth [is because of] being with her. I didn't like it at the beginning because he was so whiny and wimpy, but by the end I fell in love with him. That's typical. I liked that he realized these new things about himself as he discovered her. I think people need to be more equal in relationships and in the beginning he wasn't carrying his weight in a relationship and he learned to do it. The girl earned his trust and learned to trust. They both passed the tests! Which is a common theme in the romances I like. . . . Plus the boy learns about who she is and then will stand up for her.

There's an important lesson in the romance, in part about the achievement of reciprocity, but the pleasure Kylie describes comes not so much from learning it but from experiencing the learning of the characters.

Kylie directly addressed the notion that romances are formulaic or that the pleasure of reading them is lessened because one knows the ending. Her engagement with new characters is what keeps romances fresh for Kylie:

> Every romance is different because the people are different. The story is not in the ending, but in the way that they *get to* that ending . . . where they really know and really love each other. The struggle from attraction through problems to love [is] what makes the story.

She continued:

> The [heroine] has to make things clear to her love, and usually has to organize things . . . for them to be together which she has to do one step at a time because usually things are pretty complicated! And then they have to really see and really care about each other—hopefully forever hopefully forever. HEA [Happily Ever After], baby!

HEA indeed. Kylie takes deep pleasure in experiencing a resolution well-earned, earned through the movement from simple-consciousness to complex consciousness to enlightened consciousness, aptly illustrated by the story of Psyche and Eros.

Kylie is so deeply involved in that movement that her reading has a sensory dimension:

> [Reading romances] teaches me not to take people for granted. [I'm reminded:] To see the specialness of people and moments of connection, feel their specialness, and not take special moments and events for granted, but really REALLY experience it, enjoy it, sense it.

Jaycee also spoke of her reading as having a sensory dimension:

> I know bad things happen in life, but I love reading about people who have survived the bad things and still love each other . . . who will work through the challenges. Reading romances allows you to get to know good people, and to root for them. You get sad with them and happy with them and you cheer them on all the way. It's like guys with a sports team. When the [heroine] wins, you feel like you win, too. And you do, really, and it shows you that you can win, too!

Jaycee and Kylie don't just read romances, they feel them.

Jaycee talked about how the plot structure of historical romances heightened the play pleasure:

> Success is sweeter for them [the characters]. . . . [Historical romances] are about waiting—and anticipation. Things are doubly emotional—you are waiting and waiting but that makes things working out all the sweeter.

In the first sentence, Jaycee is talking about the characters. But in the second sentence, we see a shift to the reader. Because the romantic resolution is put off, the pleasure Jaycee derives from it has a longer duration, and when it finally occurs it is all the greater in intensity. Here is another way her reading is play: She is not imposed on by the text, she is transacting with it, actively operating on the text to extract pleasure and make meaning. She is playing with it.

Another aspect of play pleasure for our informants is that while they are reading they are in a world of endless possibilities. Here's Jaycee again: "They [romances] are just grown up fairy tales that tell you something true and give you hope. . . . They make me feel like I did when I was young and reading Cinderella."

After 9/11, romance author Cindy Gerard gave up on her writing, but then re-embraced it precisely because she feels romances provide the kind of hope Jaycee describes. As Gerard explains on her website (http://www.cindygerard.com/):

> Now more than ever, the world needs validation that good wins over evil. That there can be "happily ever afters." That love heals and love gives strength. So I started writing again . . . about strong men and women overcoming the worst life could throw at them. And I know now that I'm providing not only entertainment, but a service, if you will.

That service is, in part, providing a playful escape from the everyday, and in part, offering guidance and inspiration to work through the inevitable challenges, as Psyche was able to do.

In short, our informants were drawn to romances because of the pleasure of play, the intense lived-through immersive pleasure the girls received while they were reading. The jumping from one book by a favorite author immediately to the next was a way to extend that pleasure. But play pleasure was closely aligned with inner work pleasure, as we've just seen, and play was not the only kind of pleasure they experienced.

The Pleasure of Work

While our participants talked at length and eloquently about the pleasure of entering and experiencing the story world, they talked even more movingly about the pleasure they derive from the inner work of reading. Kylie explained how these pleasures of play and work are related:

> I love that moment when they [the hero and heroine] did something to progress the relationship along—that is the plot of a romance! It is so cutesy to me, such a jolt! There is no map provided—I don't mean a strict progression

> but there has to be a progression, development. And the development is the people getting to know each other and drawing out the best in each other . . . . The progression is getting to know each other, further deep understandings that go beyond what a friend would know—it is a best friend kind of knowledge. There are layers of acquaintances, friends, best friends, and then your partner and there are things only your partner knows—and you love each other despite the fact that you know everything about each other, including things others wouldn't know. . . . It's a lot about becoming good, becoming better because of each other and for each other.

The jolt Kylie experiences provides the impetus for a consideration about what becoming better entails and this relates to the value of seeing the big picture and being far-sighted that we see in Psyche.

In a 2012 interview with *USA Today*, romance author Robyn Carr makes a similar point:

> *One of the things romance fiction requires is admirable characters—at least the central characters. They don't always start that way, but they always get there. It takes goodness to create goodness, so there is always a reward for treating another human being with fairness, courtesy, love, and respect. Varying degrees of commitment are examined. This kind of lesson in human behavior can be a driving force in creating and maintaining relationships of all kinds. And once again, romance novels show us glaring examples of what doesn't work in any relationship—deceit, selfishness, vengeance, etc. Romance novels are all about good behavior, and strength of character equals good results. Bingo—that seems to work in real life as well. How about that?*

Here's Kylie in response to a question about what books have stayed with her, illustrating that romances can indeed be a driving force in becoming a better person and that the pleasure of inner work is both an intense and lasting one:

> In *Paper Towns* by John Green, one of my favorites, the major character is pining after this girl Margot who disappears and he has to deal with it. I felt like a better person for having read it. I felt tingly. I picked up another book and I wasn't ready. I had to wait and mourn longer. Digest it for a couple days. For this one, it wasn't the romance that stayed with me. It was that Margot felt trapped in this place. And angsty and stir crazy and I could relate to that. And it stuck with me that she just left. And it helped me to see how

> this affected the people she left. And I felt less like I have to go now and more appreciative of the people around me and how we affect each other. And that it is not the place that makes something tolerable but you and how you choose to be. I guess this [book] was a kind of anti-romance but I really liked it.

What she liked was the personal psychological work, the working through of inner challenges that it allowed her to do, and the sense of connectedness and relatedness to community that was promoted by doing it. So the inner work contained an element of social pleasure.

Kylie did far more work than this through her reading. Here she is again:

> [Reading romances] is like thinking about how you want to be loved, but also how you want to love. And seeing that it [loving relationships] will have its challenges but that you can get it. It's . . . luxurious to think about really.

There is something more going on here, though, as Kylie made clear:

> You see yourself in the heroine, so you see your best possible self or some version of it. And you see the good but also the possibilities in others, despite their shortcomings, because the hero has to be helped, transformed in some way. And you do, too, really, so the book helps you think about this and consider it.

These quotes highlight the inner work of transformation as well as the social pleasure of relatedness and helping each other through relationship and community.

And more inner work:

> "[Romance teaches that] you can be imperfect but still have moments of perfection." And again: "That's a central issue of life, maybe THE central issue—what is love? How do you get it? How do you give it? How do you negotiate the problems?"

A bit later in the discussion of dealing with relational problems, she asked: "Do you go after it [the problem] directly or indirectly, right away or over time?"

For Kylie, romances provide a way for her to explore, as Psyche did, what it means to engage in a developing relationship over time.

Seeing your best self in another person relates very clearly to Jung's notions of psychological projection. Though projection is generally considered to be a scapegoating measure, as seeing one's faults in another, Jung also goes to great lengths to show that we often fail to recognize our own repressed strengths by projecting them onto others (hero worship being a kind of example). Kylie projects her developing capacities onto the heroine and lives through further development with her.

She wasn't alone. Here's Jaycee:

> Romances are about identity, about being something and something strong, for sure. And about seeing there are different ways to be in the world and different ways of relating to other people. And you don't want to be too extreme in the way you are being—being too extreme in any one direction is not good for you or for your relationship.

Two of the girls Jeff talked to in the romance reading groups identified as lesbian. They complained that there were no lesbian romances, and so they read traditional romances and imagined they were lesbian romances. Despite having to do this kind of translating, the romances allowed them to do a similar kind of work. "You can learn the same things about relationships. You just have to use a little imagination," said one girl. "[Traditional romance] can help you think about your lesbian sexuality—in a safe and approved of way," said another.

One of the lesbian readers continued:

> I read hetero romances because that's all there is. I want books that are not about sex or lust but [are] really about love and they ride off into the sunset and are happy—real happiness is about compromise and getting through experiences together. That is really true of lesbians, too. I mean, who would choose to be this way—you are going to have extra troubles . . . . So you are going to have so much extra trouble with the world that you have to be true to each other. So I read them [the traditional romances] as mirrors. It's about a combination of friends and romantic partners who are willing to compromise because they love the other person's absolute . . . soul. You can't demand what only you want. You have to appreciate the other perspective and you have to be willing to try new things for your partner. You have to be able to invent your relationship together.

When asked the major life lessons she's learned from reading romances, she replied with a wisdom that belied her years:

> Love can wait, but not forever. Love overcomes obstacles but not all obstacles. There are things that are not beneficial in a relationship, like being too distant from each other, or not caring enough, or not [being] willing to change.

Once again our informants' responses resonated with those of romance writers. The following is from romance author Marianne Beach at galtime.com in response to the question "What can romance novels tell us about ourselves or our relationships?"

> *Romances teach us what we like and what we don't like. This sounds simplistic or obvious, but think about it this way: Romances are about intimacy, relationships, and emotions—what Nora Roberts calls a "hat trick of easy targets." When you read about people who appeal to you emotionally or intellectually, you've identified something that you like—and you can probably identify that same trait in the people you like. Nowhere is this idea more evident than in the sexuality present in romances. There are few places where women can learn about their own sexuality safely, without judgment or rampant airbrushing. But in romances, the female experience, both emotional and physical, is front and center. Romances are about women's lives, in all their variations, so readers see pieces of themselves reflected in the romances they read. It's easy to learn from that experience.*

But don't romances also teach women that their only happiness can come from a man? Don't they teach relational and sexual submission? Not according to our informants. For Kylie, a romance has to contain a sense of agency and possibility, particularly the possibility of transformation—transformation of self *and* other:

> It's about motivation and willingness. About being able to go after what you want. Valuing someone else's happiness and who they really are—what they really need—deep down—even discovering that or uncovering it for them because they don't know it or maybe even deny it. It's getting some and giving some. Truthful and authentic—it's real. There are problems to work through. You can smell an untrue romance a mile away . . . if it's too easy or natural than it's untrue.

And again our readers were very much in line with the authors of romances. Here's Sarah Wendell (2013) delineating three lessons that romances can teach:

- *That you must be the heroine of your own life. You are worthy of love and happiness . . . but finding your "happy ever after" is your responsibility. It doesn't just show up in the driveway and ring the doorbell.*

- *That being able to recognize a good partner and a good friend and relate to them are invaluable skills that improve with time and experience.*

- *That happy endings take work, require problem solving and optimism, but are attainable for everyone.*

Our informants seemed to have learned these lessons. They side with David Pollard (2005) who argues:

Romances are, in fact, subversive literature: They encourage women to be dissatisfied with inequality, and to set higher expectations for themselves, and they show them ways to achieve those expectations, largely by taming men and, in a way, usurping their power. Romances are arguably the only art form of any kind that portrays women as equal partners with men.

Perhaps we shouldn't have been surprised about the various creative ways our informants used romances to do various kinds of work. After all, it's been 30 years since Janice Radway's (1984) groundbreaking study of avid women romance readers. Radway's readers, all involved in homemaking, used their reading in many ways—as a shield that bought them a few moments of respite during the day; as a confirmation of their work as mothers, wives and nurturers; as a tool to invigorate and ready themselves for the daily tasks of nurturing and running a household. Radway explains that her informants chose to read novels that fabricated a predictable, happy ending and that depicted a heroine who discovers her own individuality through her ability to care for others, as opposed to unique personal qualities or a unique agenda of her own in the world. This confirmed and celebrated the life choices of the informants and helped them to cope with the constraints of their social world.

Kylie had no patience for those who dismissed romances, though she herself dismissed one popular instantiation of the genre:

> People who criticize romances have never read them. Or they think they are just the hot and heavy breathing kind of Harlequin romance. I read deep romances and I consider romances where people don't have problems and don't change each other and themselves to be really shallow . . . [Romances] should wake you up to special moments and to moments of challenge and psych you up to meet them.

The responses of the romance readers resonated with Dissanayake's (1988) ideas about art as "making special"—making everyday life special and considered. This process is much more nuanced and realistic, it seems to us, than blind idealism. The girls were after a real love with a real human being—and they wished in turn to be appreciated as a real human being. They understood this to be a challenge and a struggle as well as promising potentially powerful rewards, the only ones we can perhaps hope for on this earth. They willingly embraced the heroine's journey through complex consciousness.

We saw earlier in this chapter the archetypes of Tristan and Iseult the Fair and Iseult of the White Hands. It is clear that these girls do not want to be regarded as or become Iseult the Fair; they are after real love between real people. They privilege becoming and being related to as Iseult of the White Hands. They are willing to do the work of Psyche and expect that commitment to be reciprocated by Eros taking on responsibility for the relationship as well.

Social Pleasures

As you saw in our previous chapter, we have identified different kinds of social pleasures that come from reading. One involves using reading to understand and affiliate with others, and part of this, as we've already seen above, is living through and coming to understand the experiences and successes of characters. The second is to use reading to make a place for ourselves in the world. Kylie experienced both types of social pleasure through her reading of romances. Here's what she said about how her reading of romances fostered social connections: "I do like to read what others read so I can talk with them about it." She continued by explaining her experience reading *The Perks of Being a Wallflower* by Stephan Chbosky:

> I heard favorable reviews—my friends liked it and I wanted to talk to them about it. I have a book box of stuff I've picked up or people have given to me. Before I start [reading] I think about what is going on in my life right then and whether the pre-reading and thumbing through strikes me that [this particular book] is going to be helpful. I'm usually pretty picky and I won't read something unless it is really coming at me. I mean, there are enough books out there.

She was very cognizant of the importance of sharing:

> Sharing. I do it in person, for sure. And blogs. I read in public places and will read out loud to people around me. I sit with friends and read. I sit in the [school] lounge and read. I mostly read and sleep—my two biggest activities. I talk with friends about reading. I don't like book clubs—too much like school—YOU HAVE TO READ THIS BOOK TO PARTICIPATE. Gah. I have met with friends every Friday afternoon and we just talked about whatever we were reading. We helped each other find new books and read in deeper ways more than school ever did.

Even as she speaks about how reading develops social connections, she points out that her reading also always helps her to do a kind of identity work. Romances allow her to name herself as a "bookish" person and a reflective one as well.

> All around me, I hang out with bookish people and we are always trading books and we ask how we are feeling and what we are going through and we suggest books based on current needs as well as preferences, like not liking vulgarity. People say what they liked, what they are feeling or going through right now, and we suggest books. It seems to me school could be more like this.

It is obvious to us that there is a lot to value here although neither of us are romance readers. Still, both of us want to love and be loved. We believe that love, as the poet Walt Whitman has written, is the healing and redeeming power of the universe.

We also know how hard it is to maintain love relationships. We saw the same recognition in our participants. They experienced the pleasure of play very intensely by entering story worlds and living through characters they had come to care about. They experienced the long-lasting pleasure of doing crucially important psychological work. Our participants didn't talk about intellectual pleasure. Romances to them did not provide a challenge to figure things out. But they did provide, according to our informants, both the challenge of becoming a better, more whole and more related person and some sense of possible ways to achieve this. They also provided distinct social pleasure, both in terms of making connections with others and in differentiating themselves from those who didn't read or reflect on relationships in the ways that they did.

WHAT WE CAN LEARN FROM OUR ROMANCE READERS

We asked Kylie directly what advice she would give to teachers in regards to romance reading. She began by asking:

> Why do teachers stigmatize certain kinds of texts? I know there is a lot of crap. There is a lot of crap romance. But this disregards that there is crap of every genre! On every shelf! Teachers, if they take these not so great books and stigmatize the whole genre, that is a problem. But even if it is bad—like *Twilight*—there is so much that could be discussed and critiqued. Like why kids like it. That could be discussed and critiqued. And here's another thing: I think reading badly written books can help you be a better writer because you can look at the writing. You can have points of comparison. I really hate Nicholas Sparks but I read his books and all his awkward dialogue so I can see what not to do.

We've argued elsewhere (Smith, Wilhelm, & Fredricksen, 2012) that evaluative arguments are an important kind of literary argument. Romances, according to Kylie, are the perfect vehicle for encouraging that kind of argumentation.

When asked about whether romance novels could be included in school, Kylie commented:

> John Green novels would be great in school. Girls like them but they are more than YA, more than romance. Those labels have stigmas behind them for teachers and for boys. But boys would read John Green. Or maybe you can say, "You read one of ours and see what you think—talk to the girls about romance—and we'll read one of yours and say what we think." But make it a John Green kind of romance. That would be cool and enlightening and different. And romance as a theme would be great to bring into school and it shouldn't cause any problem. Another thing is that a lot of books, like vampire books and adventure books also have romance elements in them but you don't have to call them romances.

Why shouldn't we allow students to read and share one of "theirs" for every book they read of "ours?" Doesn't seem like too much to ask. Doing so would allow everyone in the classroom to learn from each other and would certainly widen the choices available. And why not read what we consider to be less rich texts paired with richer texts? Then students could compare the texts and their experiences. That would give us a lot of information to think with as teachers. Such a process would allow students to identify themselves as readers through the kinds of reading they love and enjoy. In our *Reading Don't Fix No Chevys* study (2002), one of the particular challenges was that our informants did not see themselves as readers if they did not read and enjoy what was assigned in school, even if they were avid readers of other kinds of texts. If we want our students to identify as readers, become lifelong readers, and read a variety of texts for different purposes, then we must do something to challenge the status quo.

It shouldn't be hard to include what kids are reading in our curricula, as Kylie said:

> Teachers should think of how these books could be on-topic instead of off-topic of what they are teaching. Love is part of the human experience and these books can teach how relationships work and should work and can go wrong. This is a conversation teachers should be having [with students]! There is like a divide between schools and life. It's like teachers don't want to do the things that are most interesting. [They] see it as inappropriate. They teach to the test and not what is necessary to life. Parents might not want their kids to read certain things. Because they have gay people in them, or have magic. I've smuggled lots of books

> to my friends. Teachers and parents get in the way when they try to control their kids. But the effect is for kids not to read at all, or to rebel and read what the parent disapproves of. There is no conversation this way—no give and take.

Parents should also pay heed, according to Kylie:

> Parents, the books might not be conventional but there are underlying themes and questions your kids need to deal with, and are important to talk about, and a lot of the messages in these books are really good.

Kylie makes a persuasive case that parents and teachers need to value students' choices, grant that they might know best what they need, and provide opportunities not only for independent reading and small interest group reading, but for reflection on their experiences with the texts that mean so much to them.

What can be gained from providing some choice and breaking down the walls between students' in-school and out-of-school reading? Kylie saw a contrast between her romances and the books she was forced to read in school:

> I gritted my teeth and read them—most of them. There is an element of being forced to do something and resisting that. But most of the books were not relatable to my real life, though surprisingly *To Kill a Mockingbird* I liked, and *Kite Runner*—they felt like things that affected my life, but most of them didn't.

We know that in our own out-of-school reading, we read what we want or need to, not what we're told to. Kylie would like the same privilege:

> There are times when books speak to me, times in my life when I need particular books. *Twilight* spoke to me when I read it. I needed it right then. *Paper Towns* was exactly what I needed at that time. *Twilight* was a quick read; it drew me in. I read it in two days. At that point I was a freshman in high school and I felt unloved and alone. And if Edward loved Bella he could love me, too. I think the Oatmeal (a fan website) was right—she is nondescript so the reader can imagine she is her—not too skinny, not too fat—she could be a million different people. They filmed the movie near my town and my friend and I went to be extras. They said we looked like Bella. But everyone looks like Bella! Bella is not described in an advanced way. She was me. The book made me feel the possibility of love, despite challenges. My mom really critiqued the book—I forced her to read it—and she said this is not what romance is like—

which is how I feel now—but when I read it I liked it. She [Bella] is just a plot device, not a deep person.

Here's another consideration: The next generation of standards and assessments throughout the world call for teachers to help students do what experts do in the ways that experts do them. In cognitive science this is called meeting the *correspondence concept* (Bereiter, 2004)—that everything that is learned should result in learners' developing attitudes and strategies that correspond to those of experts. If expert adult readers exercise choice and pursue the reading they feel that they need and that can help them at a particular moment, and if experts evaluate and compare the meaning, effects, and value of different texts, then why shouldn't students?

The role of this kind of choice was central to Kylie:

School tells us to read books, because "everyone" has read them. Because you are expected to know them. I much prefer book lists where you make a choice. Not everyone likes the same books. I can take a list to [my] librarian and discuss what would be the best match for me. And my librarian knew me and helped me find the books I needed.

The reading of romances worries us considerably less now than before the study. For these girls, reading romance was an exercise in sharing and widening textual choices and responses, in deep reading, in supporting each other's reading. Their reading and sharing was about exploring the psychology and tactics of love, commitment, relationship and relatedness, and sexuality in a very contained and safe way.

The books themselves seem to provide what depth psychologists call *containers* for strong feelings and desires; that is, they provide a way to place hold, contain, study, and reflect upon something that provides so much emotion and energy that it is otherwise dangerous to experiment with and consider in real-life contexts. Containers offer a safe way to bring the unconscious into consciousness.

The two of us have long argued that motivation is a primary challenge facing teachers, if not the primary one. And we have also argued for "going with the flow" (Smith & Wilhelm, 2002; 2006) by following our students' interests and energies and bridging from these to more sophisticated texts and complex thinking. So why not go with our student readers' passions and get them to share their books and responses with others? This would help to create a community of readers that other students might be willing to join.

That said, it seems paramount to us that teachers also provide opportunities and mechanisms for reflection, opportunities to consider how reading the genre might be healthy, but also how it might be dangerous or reasonably critiqued, how it might feed into patriarchal stereotypes. All of these are significant and profound topics for our students and for us to consider. Romances clearly provide an opportunity to do just that.

CHAPTER 8

The Lure of Immortality

Going Batty for Vampire Novels

In the previous chapter we took a close look at the nature and variety of the pleasures experienced by committed readers of romance. Play pleasure and social pleasure were surely important to these readers, but the pleasure of doing the kind of inner work privileged by depth psychologists seemed even more significant. Kylie, our chief respondent, was very clear that these pleasures derived from reading "real" romances, and she questioned whether the Twilight series qualified as romance. Whether it does or not, vampire stories are clearly enormously popular with young readers, so we thought we'd devote some attention to that genre.

Why Vampire Books?

We began this study with a desire to look at the reading of texts that seem to make many adults uneasy. Vampire stories involve the paranormal and supernatural activity, witchery, and implicit and occasionally explicit sex and violence—which many adults, including ourselves, find disturbing.

The vampire archetype and story are primordial in almost every culture, including the earliest recorded epic of *Gilgamesh* from Babylonia in about 2000 B.C. In *Gilgamesh*, the Ekimmu, or Departed Spirit, was the soul of a dead person who could not find rest and wandered over the earth seeking to seize the living.

Subsequent to *Gilgamesh,* the vampire appeared in fairy and folk tales across the world. The vampire image and vampire stories are incredibly diverse. However, as all with archetypes, there are standard structural features that unite these stories. For instance, vampires once were perfectly normal human beings who lost their wholeness, some aspect of their spiritual or moral nature, particularly the ability to generate their own purpose and life energy. This is typically the result of some unfortunate incident or series of events. Another common feature is that vampires extract life from others and this is how they maintain themselves. It's commonly understood that this is done by sucking blood from a victim, but in fact there are many vampire stories in which life is sucked through infection, possession, or some kind of psychic draining

Ernest Jones, in his famous work *On the Nightmare* (1931), explicitly states that the vampire operates as an archetype on both the individual/personal level and the collective/cultural level: "The two chief metaphorical connotations of the word [vampire] are: 1) a social or political tyrant/force who sucks the life from the people . . . [and] 2) an irresistible lover who sucks away energy, ambition, or even life for selfish reasons" (cited in Carter, 1988, p. 151). Pretty scary. But as we'll see, pretty pleasurable as well.

The Pleasure of Play in Reading About Vampires

Vampire stories provided their readers the pleasure of play, which, as we've seen, derives from entering a story world so fully that readers feel as though they are actually experiencing it. Here's Allie, one of our two primary vampire respondents talking about the Twilight books:

> What draws people to *Twilight* is that it is relatable. Young characters. Teenagers. Relationships. Love. The dangers of love. You need it [love] so bad but it is dangerous and can slay you. That's the interest of teenage girls. Feelings—Bella's feelings can be related to. So intense. Most of what I read in school I cannot relate to. Like George Orwell's *1984*. There was NOTHING I could relate to. I wasn't interested in entering into the story. But I am so interested in entering into *Twilight* because it is about me right now. I can relate to it.

Entering the world of the Twilight books involves immersive play pleasure, but in service to social pleasure in regards to relationship with the self. What makes Bella's feelings so intense, more intense than a typical romance? Allie explained:

> I would definitely say *Twilight* is a [paranormal] romance. The vampire thing is just a side story—an intensifier. It makes Edward more interesting and dangerous. And his competition with Jacob [a werewolf] has higher stakes [because he's a vampire]. It has to do with him [Edward] being a monster to some people and having the possibility of going demonic. So it makes the romance more intense and enjoyable.

She continued:

> The immortal thing is really riveting—knowing that is not possible for us. So that is fascinating and interesting. It means he [Edward] is endless. He doesn't age. He doesn't change. When Bella becomes a vampire they can love each other forever. That is so cool. That is such an appeal. To stay that age—Edward is 17 she is 19 or something—things are not going to change. In real life, time changes you. There are so many things that come with age that are not that great—but they [Edward and Bella] are timeless and it is always going to be love and youth for them and timelessness and endless possibility.

And further:

> If there are vampires, the situations and plot and feelings are going to be really extreme—some of that has to do with timelessness, deathlessness, foreverness of being immortal. Everything is bigger and has more consequence. I mean Edward is going to be with Bella for all of time!

Kennie, our second main vampire informant, also saw the Twilight books as romance novels. She was a reader of what she considered to be more traditional vampire stories because she felt the classic vampire stories provide a richer play pleasure:

> *Twilight* is okay but not my favorite. It's a vampire book that is not for vampire readers. I enjoy it as a rom-com [romantic comedy]. Stephanie Meyer took a lot of liberty with the myths and legends. And her characters don't develop. In the vampire stories, I like how the vampire develops and transforms because of his relationship with a woman. I like the Vampire

> Academy series by Rochelle Mead. There is more going on than falling in love. I like that. You are still moving through life and fighting off the evil vampires, meeting challenges, doing what you have to do, so your life is not the romance, it is having a relationship that enriches your life and helps you do all the things you are already doing. It's not one-track mind stuff where it is all about romance. It is about enriching each other and helping each other to live your lives. It is satisfying to me if it is a friendship thing. If it is just romance, it doesn't stick with me; I don't feel the characters are real. It's only fulfilling while reading, but not afterwards. I want something that sticks with me and helps me think about my life over time.

You can see here that Kennie was engaging in immersive play pleasure, but that she expected this to involve and lead to other pleasures. She expects the reading not only to provide the pleasure of play in the moment but also, as we'll see in greater detail, to offer work and intellectual pleasures after the story has been read. We can also see that the duration of pleasure is important to her—the longer the better.

Kennie also believed that the theme of immortality intensified the experience of reading:

> Mortal characters can sometimes stay mortal no matter what a vampire does to them. Usually there are rules the vampires follow—like they will only change someone [into a vampire] who is near death with no chance of help. And this will [happen] only if they have a close connection, or the love interest. It's always pretty extreme and intense when someone is going to become a vampire. Big.

This intense engagement with characters, both vampires and humans, was one of the primary pleasures Kennie took from her reading:

> I love Kressley Cole—I like her vampires and I like her other characters. I've read 15 of her series books—lots of intertwining characters—they [the characters] keep reappearing. One book helps you understand the next book. With most novels, you are just done. But in these novels you will learn more about the characters, you get to relate to them over time. It just makes you want to keep reading and to see how they will develop. I get great satisfaction out of the character development.

The Pleasure of Doing Inner Work

As important as the pleasure of play was to our readers, the pleasure of doing inner work seemed even more significant to them. For these girls, the vampire stories captured the possibility of transformative experiences, of becoming more alive through relationship— with their deep selves and their own animus energy as well as with a romantic partner. Like the romance readers, there seems an urge towards wholeness and integration, and of taming and incorporating the male animus energy—both in oneself and in the world.

Considering Relationships

One kind of inner work the vampire stories let our informants do was considering the kind of relationship they wanted to enter. Jaycee, who we met last chapter, was a reader of the Twilight series. Her comments about the books are relevant here:

> Being a teenager is partly about struggling to be more adult and have more adult relationships . . . . I think a real struggle of more adult relationships is making sure they are life-giving in both directions. I mean, we all have these needs so you have to be careful about not being a vampire and sucking someone else dry, or hurting and discarding them. But you have to be really careful not to let someone do it to you, too, like dominate you, just because you like being liked or feeling attractive or whatever. I think it's a real danger.

Jaycee uses the vampire books to reflect on the very real work of undertaking more mature, adult, reciprocal relationships and not getting sucked into one-way relationships.

Allie also used the books to reflect on the importance of reciprocity:

> I love vampires in love stories—it adds this extreme element that is so cool. Edward is constantly fighting against his instincts. With Bella he sees her and just wants to eat her. So he really has to put away his instinct to be around her, get to know her, she is so different to him. That uncertainty is interesting. Can he do it—for her? Can he overcome himself for the sake of relationship? The fact that she is such a Plain Jane but he loves her and is in awe of her, that kind of makes the reader feel like if I am plain it is possible that someone can love me that way, will see through me to the real me even the coolest guy and he will protect me instead of using me. There are so many uncertainties, love is a leap of faith. This is a double leap [in *Twilight*] because

> of his instinct. He struggles with that the whole time. But he overcomes the animal instinct to love Bella. It's almost like he becomes admirably human in some ways. He has to sacrifice being comfortable to love her. That is what makes it so special. As the saga goes on he gets more relaxed and it is not that big of a deal but in the beginning that is so crucial and obvious. You have to rein in your power to get love, become human, get the ultimate satisfactions—vampire stories really show that and that is why I love them.

So did Kennie:

> Vampires can play "hard to get" on one hand and they are willing to really work hard to get their woman on the other—I mean, that is more attractive than just waiting and wanting for it all to happen.

And later:

> Most of the time I have trouble with the vampires' values—they are so old world, male-centered—but as the book progresses they will become less so to a manageable state.

Allie made a strikingly similar remark:

> The vampires are almost "old school" and I like how they are not like the boys I know but more mature and gentlemanly. But that also puts me off—it's kind of weird but I guess it scares me. You know there is something they are hiding.

The girls' comments resonate with Hyder's (2001) contention that the vampire archetype symbolizes the dangers of a one-sided relationship:

> *The vampire offers us a mirror of one-sided relationships within the individual, between people, and between ourselves as a species and our environment and God-image. . . but it is also a reminder that we can discover new life from death and despair . . . . We can be transformed [through relationship] into darkness or into wholeness and light. (p. 1)*

The agent of that transformation is a woman, and our readers clearly embraced that transformative power. Here's Kennie:

> Females in female vampire books work for good and they get their vampire to do the same. . . . The difficulties in *Twilight* stem from Edward and these

> are psychological differences with Bella that are too big to overcome—he is too big, needy, in love, fast, old, different—he feels it [the relationship with Bella] will only end badly. That he has no soul and the only way for it to work is for him to have a soul. He *does* believe in a god. The main vampires believe in souls and they don't have souls so they feel they must have lost them. In *Twilight*, Bella believes that Carlyle is right—that though [the vampires] are immortal and inherently bad, they *can* redeem themselves—they did not really lose their souls, only their humanity—they can go to heaven, they can get back in touch with their souls, but they need help.

Part of the pleasure here, it seems to us, is in rooting for the female protagonist to provide the help that is needed, or to put yourself in her place acting as an agent on behalf of the vampire, trying to redeem him.

We can see Kennie's identification clearly:

> Sometimes things seem bleak and insurmountable, in life and in relationships, like there's always mountains beyond the mountain . . . . You want so much and it just aches. You want it to go good but it could go bad. So you want to know what will make it good. . . . Maybe that's why I like [vampire novels] where the heroine is able to turn the vampire into a man who can love her without smothering and killing her.

Kennie's comment resonates with Hyder's (2001) contention that "the vampire is the unrealized, repressed and therefore undead and destructive archetype of the potential 'true man'" (p. 13).

Kennie, in fact, wants other, younger readers to experience the same kind of identification:

> In general, romance readers like vampire [books] and vampire readers like romances. There is a lot of crossover. Both are about forbidden romance. There are masculine vamp novels and female vamp novels. Female ones always involve romance to some degree, the question is how much. I haven't read too many male ones—they are more about darkness, war and death, conquering hero, fighting. [The female books are about] vampire-human relationships, but one of them [the characters] can be a vampire-halfling, an elf, there can be witch relationships. But it's always about love that overcomes differences and makes the lovers something more. The newer books, especially for younger readers, are giving the females more power— and I like that.

Considering Sexuality

Sex, of course, is part of healthy relationships. And although our readers didn't talk much about how sex and sexuality are treated in their books, what they did say was revealing. Here's Allie:

> On one level vampires can do whatever they want, and that is appealing and scary. When it comes to anything but, of course, when it comes to sex . . . that Edward is controlling this [his sexual urges] makes him approachable, potentially redeemable.

And Jaycee teasingly commented:

> Sex is kind of dangerous, you know. Or haven't you heard? . . . Reading about sexual attraction doesn't make it more dangerous. In fact, it can help you see positive possibilities for real healthy relationships.

Kennie pointed out that the constructive effort of reading in fact requires readers to imagine those possibilities:

> There is a real fantasy element to just being totally loved and being needed, like a vampire needs the heroine to stay alive—literally and symbolically. Sex is part of that, but usually that's more implied and imagined than directly talked about. I think that makes it [the sexual tension and energy] more powerful. There's this kind of restraint, I guess. I think that makes it even better because it is totally up to your imagination and anything can happen.

In our last chapter we discussed what depth psychologists call containers for strong feelings and desires, and how books can provide a way to safely contain and reflect upon something that may be dangerous to experiment with or consider in real-life contexts. Kennie's comment suggests that vampire stories provide containers for the consideration of sexuality.

The kind of consideration in which the girls engaged depended on their agency (Wilhelm, 2008). As you've seen throughout the book, our various informants have indicated a desire to become a creative/creating participant in the story, to rewrite scenes, or to fill in gaps, to write fanfics. This kind of agency leads to a kind of inner work. It provides what Santayana calls "imaginative rehearsals for living" (cited in Booth, 1983, p. 212). Johnson (1992) notes that "One feminist interpretation sees Bram Stoker's *Dracula* as a myth of feminine liberation and empowerment. Through her encounter with the vampire, Lucy changes from a silly, giggly girl to a powerfully erotic woman." This viewpoint definitely captured something of the girls' responses.

Being Powerful

The girls' interest in power went far beyond the sexual arena. They read vampire novels in part as narratives of female empowerment more generally. Here's Allie:

> I don't think there is a lot of pro-feminism in the Twilight series—until in the last book once Bella becomes a vampire and is able to take care of herself and her family. It's the "damsel in distress" thing until the final book. She is pretty helpless until she becomes a vampire. She cuts herself to save Edward and that is a powerful thing and a thing saving her as well as him. She gets to the point that she can protect herself and live the way she wants. . . . I really hated how pathetic [Bella] was until that point, so I was like, "Yeah!"

She continued: "Just look at everything that Bella went through, yet she survived. I think that tells about her female strength. . . . She moved from totally weak to totally strong, as a female."

Kennie looked for a similar kind of movement:

> I like strong females and I take an interest in the development of female characters in becoming strong. . . . My fave character is Emma from Kresley Cole's Immortals After Dark books—half-vampire, half Valkyrie. She is very interesting in her development from shy to respected and dominant figure in the whole series. She becomes very powerful. She has the happy ending but there are new challenges that show unexpected developments, like there are factions going out for her and she has to develop even more.

She explained further:

> A Valkyrie is characterized as a daughter of two Norwegian deities: Woden and Freda. Valkyries are born when a victorious warrior woman is plucked off the battlefield—they are fierce and dominating. They are like a female vampire in their powers but they abhor vampires. It causes a problem for her [Emma] that she is half-vampire. This part of her is disdained so she is separated from the Valkyrie race. . . but she is strong and she can take it. And she really is more Valkyrie than vampire. . . . It makes you think about what determines who you really are and why people judge you on background instead of who you really are.

Note her move in the last sentence from the book to her own life. Sharon, our research assistant, pointed out to us how frequently our student readers moved from talking about a book to reflecting on their own lives. Our readers were engaged deeply in the story world and that engagement enabled them do important inner work.

Being Rebellious

As Senf (1988) points out, "Dracula is dangerous because he expresses his contempt for authority in the most individualistic of ways" (p. 94). Hyder (personal communication, 2012) also asserts that Dracula is symbolic of the ultimate defiance and rebelliousness—defiance not only of human conventions "but of death itself." He argues further that this counter-culturalism taps into teen rebelliousness, calling into question conventionality and rules, while celebrating resistance to such conventionality. Ultimately he concludes the following:

As far as what turns kids on [about vampires], I'd suggest the vampire as the outsider, the marginalized figure, the rebel, the rageful: kids feel disgust and rejection toward the hypocrisy of a morally, spiritually bankrupt, and hypocritical collective [adult role models/parents/society], and they therefore feel allied and aligned against the threat of the collective shadow, the life-sucking, parasitic, predatory nature they despise in the "above world" around them they would prefer to reject. (brackets in original correspondence)

Our girls would agree that part of the appeal of their reading was indeed allying themselves with the vampire's defiance. Here's Allie:

In the very first book Edward was a rebel—he pretty much does what he wants—he's been to high school tons of times—so he comes late, drives dangerously and fast—he just does what he wants. This is a big reason why all the vampires are idolized—cool and mysterious and rebellious—they are like the ultimate bad boys—and they are willing to take initiative and do things . . . and do things their own way.

Once again the vampire seems to offer the girls a kind of container, a liminal space for imaginatively trying out what Jung would call their shadow energies, for considering what life would be like if they broke all the rules.

But beyond the attractiveness of this rebelliousness and rule breaking, the girls also offered critiques. Here's Kennie: "All the 'doing your own thing' is attractive on one level, but it has to be brought under control. That is what the female is for, not to kill the rebelliousness but to harness it."

It's hard to imagine Jung himself saying something more spot-on about the role of anima energy in relationship with male animus energy, or the role of containers in harnessing and bringing unconscious energies into consciousness where they can be controlled and used in the process of individuation.

And when Edward becomes less of a rebel, Allie observed:

> I really like Edward and admired him and his sacrifice giving up some of his vampire tendencies and how he loved Bella. But I think he became a bit too heavy and serious. That is okay as a character but if he was real I'd tell him to lighten up. He lost some of his energy.

He lost some of the energy that Allie wants to share in.

Maintaining Control

Both of our primary informants were attracted to the danger in the characters about whom they were reading. That danger allowed them to reflect on the importance of control. Here's Allie:

> Vampires are definitely about bloodlust and repressed animal impulses that must be controlled [and] maybe recognized, which is what the vampire makes you do and has to do for himself.

Kennie made a similar comment:

> Other kinds of favorite characters are werewolves, and factions of demons. I really like range demons. They are like Valkyries. Two brothers, Ridestrom and Acadian, are range demons—they look and appear like demons with horns. They appear human but taller and more muscular. But when they go into a rage frenzy, the consequences are very dire. It's a total loss of control. . . I like *Kingdom of Werewolves* [stories] set in Scotland. I like those werewolves. They have a lot of humanity because they are in control of their werewolfishness. I also like their humor—they make a lot of body jokes, which they call BAWDY jokes, get it? They are super masculine but usually really funny, too, which takes the edge off. Their control allows them to retain some of their humanity and so are less dark.

According to Jung, conscious control, particularly of bringing elements of the shadow into the light of consciousness, is a major element of inner work. It makes what is in the shadow less dark. Again, there seems to be an implication that the girls are exploring their own strengths, how to become fully themselves and agents in the world, and how to become conscious of and exert control over previously repressed shadow energies.

The Pleasure of Figuring Things Out

Not only did the vampire stories foster inner work, they also fostered our readers' intellectual engagement in big ideas. Indeed, we found a remarkable similarity between what the girls talked about and the issues literary critics have taken up. We'll illustrate by pairing the critical responses with the girls' comments.

Good vs. Evil

Raible (1988) argues that

> Dracula *is, of course, a morality play. Forces of good and evil, clearly identified, clash until the climax and final destruction of the dread vampire. If the evil is more suave and seductive—more intelligent and attractive—than is the devil in medieval morality dramas, that may be simply an expression of modern sophistication. (p. 105)*

Allie and Kennie saw their own reading of vampire books as an exploration of the struggle between good and evil, but in a very complicated and nuanced way. Here's how Allie put it:

> The good and evil thing is worked out differently [in the Twilight books]. It's about the vampires and their struggles—not about vampires being bad versus humans being good. Which I liked because we all know humans can be evil. Edward and his family are good. The Voltury are not evil necessarily. It's complicated—to humans and in human terms they are [evil]—they trick them to eat them—but in another way the vampires are just different. This is what vampires do. But Edward's family is not like most vampires. They overcome . . . being vampires. They are a minority. The Voltury are definitely demonic. Edward's family has become not demonic but they are still in danger of it. They have to make the effort. Like all of us, I guess.

And here's Kennie:

> Most of the main vampire characters become good at least to some
> degree. Lothaire [the protagonist of the vampire novel *Lothaire* by Kresley
> Cole] starts as evil and murderous and the plot goes for three-quarters
> and then he becomes . . . well, not good, but a grayish area—ending the
> book neutral. . . So it's not like humans being good and vampires being
> bad. There is always struggle between good and evil vampires and good
> and evil within a vampire. Authors give them different species names.
> Put them in different armies. Sometimes they right out say these are
> good, these are bad, sometimes they make you figure it out and in those
> books the goodness and evilness are more complicated and that is more
> interesting and fun.

Figuring things out, dealing with complexity, Kennie says, provides an
intellectual pleasure.

Danger/Abuse

In vampire stories, danger and the threat of abusive relationships are always present.
Though the relationship can be transforming, it can also be damning. Hyder explains:

> [In vampire stories] one is reminded of the infamous Stockholm complex,
> wherein the captives, held for so long against their own will, develop a
> sympathy and even alliance with the captors, kidnappers, and their causes.
> A similar sort of perverse accommodation and loyalty develops between the
> addict and his addiction, the abused partner and her/his abuser, outside or
> within. (p. 172)

Kennie and Allie saw a similar threat. Here's Kennie: "[In vampire relationships]
there is always the danger—drawing you on, but scaring you, too. You want to be careful
but not to miss out." And Allie: "I like Edward and Bella together but he was really
controlling. Where protectiveness becomes control you have a problem."

The Repressed and the Unexplained

Part of the fascination for these readers was thinking about the unexplained, the
irrational, and by implication, with the deeply repressed—with all that Jung would say
is in the shadow—a fascination they shared with critics. Hatlan (1988) writes: "It is

'otherness' itself, all that bourgeois society has repudiated, that Dracula represents—the psychically repressed and the socially oppressed" (pp. 120-131). Wasson (1988) makes a similar comment:

Technological progress, having cut humanity off from the old superstitious, dark knowledge, makes itself increasingly vulnerable to the demonic powers like the vampire, for, having written them off as unreal, civilized man has no defense against them. (pp. 19–23)

The girls shared strikingly similar thoughts. Here's Jaycee:

You know there are things out there that you don't know about, that are mysterious and unexplained, and the vampires and werewolves and their stories make that incredibly real to you, bring it out from the dark so you can see it. Then you have to deal with it.

And Allie:

Vampires are of the past, of dangers we don't see anymore but are still there. You do kind of wonder when it is all going to explode and can't be ignored anymore. . . . I think the books are somewhat about dangers we don't see—I mean the regular people [in the Twilight series] don't know about the werewolves or the vampires but they are there. There are definitely things that people ignore or just explain away. In the Twilight books, people are oblivious. Only the reader really knows. So the reader is like the author, all-knowing, and that is cool. It just shows how we ignore problems in real life or think we know everything when we obviously don't.

Realizing that something is missing and even figuring out what most people are missing seems to be an intellectual pleasure, but it also constitutes a work pleasure as it's a move towards seeing what is repressed—and therefore, it's a move toward balance, wholeness, and completion. Any time we bring out what is repressed we are working with our individual shadow or the collective shadow.

The Nature of Adolescence

One theme our readers explored that was not touched upon by the critics is the suggestion that becoming a vampire is analogous to becoming an adolescent—possessed by new energies and urges, dependent but desiring independence or at least the desire to carry your own weight in the world and in a relationship. Kennie had this to say:

> It's fascinating to think about not being fully alive—or not fully alive yet, or not fully formed yet, and what that might be like [to be fully alive] and how to make that happen. As a teenager, as a student, you just feel kind of *in-between*. Like there are uncomfortable things you just have to go through even though you don't really want to. [Vampire books] help me to think about how other people feel like vampires, too—[and about] how you can be more fully alive, about how you make or might make others more alive, or more dead for that matter. I like the books where the woman makes the vampire more alive, brings him out of his deadness and into life.

Vampires and Politics

The girls also used their reading to reflect on political issues. Here's Jaycee:

> But the Volturys are way different. They lure groups of people into their lair or whatever you want to call it and eat them. The [victims] are blindsided. They [the Volturys] have great power and they use it to benefit only themselves and suck people dry. They don't care who and what they destroy. I could see this 1%/99% Occupy Wall Street thing with them. They are like the rich and powerful, like a corporation that is undermining everybody. But Edward's family was not part of that corporation if you see what I mean. So power doesn't necessarily mean evil or exploitation. But if you have power, you have to be really careful, which is what Edward is all about.

SOCIAL PLEASURE

Reading the books involved both the social pleasure of connecting with others and the social pleasure of naming oneself.

Connecting with Others

We've already talked about the play pleasure that the girls experienced. That pleasure had a social dimension in their awareness that other readers were experiencing a similar kind of pleasure, as Allie explained:

> You just get sucked into it—you focus just on the experience. You come to like the characters and being with them. . . . It's not like I'd want to hang out with the characters in real life but I like being with them as a reader. And I like being with other readers being with them [the characters].

Not only did their reading connect our readers to unknown others, it also connected them more deeply to their friends. Allie explained: "All of my friends love Twilight, every one of us. We read all the books. We go to the movies as soon as they come out." And we talk about them:

> Some of my friends like [Twilight] because they don't like Bella—she's just too awkward and helpless, at least at the start. It's fun to critique characters. We'll watch the movies to make fun of Bella. [As we watch] we tell her what she could do differently, [like] be stronger. It's fun to critique, to have characters to criticize, to have events you would do differently.

Even when she didn't participate with other Twilight fans, Allie recognized the social dimension of the reading of others:

> We didn't do the team thing. We are fans but not over the top. We don't buy t-shirts and all that. The Team Jacob vs. Team Edward thing—I never really got into that. It was a movie phenomenon, not a book thing, in my opinion. The whole thing started when Bella had to choose who she wanted to love. At that point, when the second film came out—that really made it happen. Book readers weren't that into it but it was a big deal for the movie. It was just a social thing. Something to argue and talk about.

Naming Oneself

Interestingly, our informants also took pleasure from the resistance of others. This resistance allowed the readers to identify themselves.

Here's Kennie:

> Parents worry that if kids play video games they will become violent. They will learn violence. That is why they worry about vampire novels—that [kids who read them] will let their sexuality take them over—or glorify the [intensity] and fall in love with someone unacceptable like a kind of crazy cross-creature romance over practicality—that they will be possessed

and not take control over their whole life—that they will be attracted by stereotypical desires and alpha males . . . . It's kind of funny but some of the fun is watching adults squirm about what you read.

However, it's important to note that Kennie kept her reading private from certain authorities she thought would not approve:

I read them privately. I don't think my teachers even know I read these things. My mom knows but she doesn't understand it, but she is a reader and so is my dad. They wish I would read other things . . . It's something to unwind. It's private. I'm little embarrassed by my interest. It is not supported by the culture. I keep it private out of necessity.

But Kennie is outspoken about the value of this reading:

People assume the stereotypes and that all of them are true. That there is no depth, all lovey-dovey, danger, sex, simple—but there is so much more to the books . . . If you read these books you are intelligent. There is a lot of deep stuff going on in them.

Even if she sometimes hides her reading preferences, she believes those preferences mark her as intelligent.

Allie, on the other hand, almost rejoiced in the insider mentality and camaraderie that was forged in the face of criticism:

So many male people say "Twilight is just so dumb." [They] can't believe you like "that crap." But we can resist them and say, "Hey we love it." We are not afraid to like it because of people who don't like it. Most of them have never read the books anyway; they just think they know what they are about. But we know and we like going back at them.

The social pleasure here is both in terms of relating to the self and to others who are allies or who are resisting her choices.

Allie continued:

Sure, being a Twilight reader identifies me. I mean when people ask you if you read Twilight it says a lot about you. People will say: "I loved it, too" and then you have this shared thing, or there is a stigma. Either way, [being a Twilight reader] is part of your identity.

Allie resisted the resistance, in so doing asserting a feminist identity:

> In English class we talked about feminist theory and I thought a lot about the Twilight books. There is a huge fan base but also a lot of critics who just so diss it. It made me think: What makes good literature? Who gets to decide? Twilight has a female fan base. Is that why it is not regarded highly by critics? It is meant to be something for women to enjoy. And I enjoy it. Isn't that good enough? I just want to stand up and say that it is good enough!

And later:

> People diss it. Why? Because girls like it? It's a way to play superior. Why do people critique it so hard? Why are the Twilight books such a lightning rod? I think there is a real critique of female books about female themes and concerns. It reminds me of how women had to use male pen names. This [Twilight] is about relationships and feelings and irrational and illogical and that is more appealing to females. Also Bella becomes stronger and less helpless. It's soft and about vulnerability and emotions and sacrifice—so it's not male . . . but it's also about females becoming stronger.

Her comment reveals a playful immersive pleasure, but that pleasure is also social because, as Jaycee maintained, part of the fun is "wanting to know what the fuss is about—being able to converse, share, and relate to others readers about it. There are chances to talk about it."

What We Can Learn from Our Vampire Book Readers

Our first response to these vampire readers is: Wow! Their reading and responses are so thoughtful and reflective. We admire the way they connected with characters, the inner work they accomplished through their reading, the deep thinking their reading inspired, and the way their reading helped them connect with others and name themselves. We see the intensity of the pleasure they felt in entering a story world and in conversing with others about those worlds. We see the long-lasting work and intellectual pleasures that they experienced and how their reading helped them name themselves.

Our data make us think about our stances and attitudes as teachers and challenge us to be more open-minded about students' reading choices. The responses of our readers steel our resolve to provide encouragement and time for free reading and to provide students time to share their reading choices and responses in various ways. They remind us to ask students why they like certain texts and to ask them how they respond because the answers can inform us and may very well surprise us.

The data from these students also made us think about our instructional strategies, especially those that are useful in helping students see the underside or untold side of a story, as so much of the girls' pleasure stemmed from that kind of seeing. Drama and action strategies seem to us to be especially good for getting at the shadow experience of characters and to bring their unconscious experience into the light. For example, the dramatic technique of *good angel/bad angel* (see Wilhelm, 2012b) in which students act as angels encouraging a character to make choices they would regard as more healthy or less healthy for them. This technique can help us look hard at what attracts us and how we should feel about that.

Another way to get after what is repressed or unrevealed about characters is the *inner voice* technique in which one student plays a character who is interviewed by the class but who withholds information from the audience or lies to them while another student stands behind the character and reveals what is really being thought and felt.

Two-sided dramas which use short role-plays or tableaux to look at a scene from a book, then translate it into the current lived experience of the students, or a real-life experience contrasted with a symbolic version, are also powerful for getting after archetypal underpinnings. (See Wilhelm, 2012b, for a full description of all these kinds of action strategies.)

That so many of our informants' responses resonated with the critical quotes we featured in this chapter suggests to us that teachers could find critical quotes about any work of literature and have students respond to these critical quotes, using these quotes as a kind of prompt for their own response, or as something to react to—explaining to what degree they agree or disagree and why. This could be done orally or in writing that is then shared in a silent discussion. Students could also be asked to respond in a similar fashion to critical events in a book. Likewise, students could find their own critical quotes that they both agree and disagree with. For this activity, it's important to use several different quotes that take different perspectives or make different judgments. We've found that the more a critical comment takes issue with students' own thinking, the more energetic the response. If some of your students are reading vampire books you could ask them to consider and respond to the critical quotes in this chapter or some of the informants' comments that are featured here.

We've learned from our friend Deb Appleman (2010) about the power of using critical theory/literary theory lenses to help students tease out the deep issues of literature and to widen and enrich their response. We know from our own experience that studying archetypal and feminist approaches to literature can be hugely useful and enlightening to students, and doing so would certainly help readers of any text, including vampire texts, to do the kind of work that the readers here are already doing. Feminism, it seems to us, is especially helpful in consciously dealing with what depth psychologists call anima and animus energy.

These readers are clearly using their favorite books to do inner work. Our readers remind us to bring inner work into the classroom by raising issues for students to write or talk about. Prompts like, "How do you see your own life and life challenges in this book?" would seem to be especially useful.

The thing to remember, we think, is the potential for inner work that such books can catalyze. That will help us value students' choices to read such books and will suggest activities that extend the positive possibilities for more complex consciousness and wide-awake and humane living offered by all of their reading.

CHAPTER 9

The Call of Horror

Containing What's in the Dark Shadows

As part of this study, Jeff surveyed 360 ninth graders in two junior high schools in different towns, one urban and one suburban, regarding their familiarity with and interest in different genres. Both schools reflect a wide range of socio-economic and ethnic diversity. The respondents were almost exactly 50/50 male/female. When Jeff asked them to rate their interest in various genres on a scale of one to ten, horror was the winner with an average score of 7.7. Fantasy was next at 7.5. No other genre scored an average over 5. Horror, construed widely, had a clear appeal to students, particularly those who were reluctant readers. Indeed, horror was so broadly popular that we decided to draw our data for this chapter from the survey responses rather than through in-depth interviews with individual readers, supplementing the survey responses with some comments from the horror aficionados among our 14 primary respondents.

We were both initially somewhat surprised by horror's popularity, maybe because we share an aversion to horror in writing or film. But reflecting back on our teaching careers, perhaps we should not have been so surprised. Both of us had students who read cartloads of YA horror authors R.L. Stine and Christopher Pike. Other authors with big followings included Joan Lowery Nixon, Caroline B. Cooney, Stephen King, V.C. Andrews, and Dean Koontz. We've long wondered, what is the appeal of horror?

Why Horror? Going Back in Time

The popularity of horror begins well before middle school. As just one example, in Boise State Writing Project Fellow Angela Housley's fourth-grade classroom, she says that "for four years running, the most popular books [in my classroom] have been Alvin Schwartz's Scary Story series. I think every kid in the class has read each and every one of the books, every year."

What's the appeal? D. W. Harding (1967) has this to say on horror's invitation to the reader:

> As in dreams, fear formulation may be as important as wish formulation. Ghost stories are likely to serve this purpose, and for children, especially, may have the therapeutic function of providing a melodramatized parallel to the child's own anxieties and then demonstrating that even these imaginary perils can be survived. (pp. 8–9)

To use a term from depth psychology that we employed in out last two chapters, one could say that Harding sees ghost stories, a subset of horror, as a psychological container for examining fears and shadow contents.

In *Encountering the Monster: Pathways in Children's Dreams,* Beaudet (1990) explores how children's unfolding experience of monsters parallel the heroic initiations of adult psychoanalysis, of undertaking the profound challenge of outgrowing oneself and becoming more whole and conscious—the purpose of inner work, and one that provides a clear form of work pleasure:

> The monster is a numinous and unknown power, and when the monster appears on the child's path, it stimulates the child to become centered and to experience and mobilize his or her own strength. The monster is also a being of metamorphosis, awakening the child who approaches it with the intelligence of the heart to that child's own creative openness and relational function. The monster finally is the engulfer, the one who swallows and brings renewed life, and it initiates the one who descends to its depths into the mystery of surrender and the perpetual regeneration of life. (p. 99)

While the monster may be experienced as a threat to the growing child's ego/current sense of self, Beaudet continues:

It may also spur the development of that ego, reinforcing its strength,
favoring its openness or regenerating it, as the child encounters the monster
and becomes immune to its dangers by taking in infinitesimal doses the
psychic force to which the monster gives form. (p. 99)

But it's not just kids. In response to the question "Why read horror?" on the horror section of the Goodreads website, one adult posted the following:

Because people are made up of feelings and passions as well as reason, and
find refreshment and entertainment on these levels. Also there is a strong
dream-like quality *about many of these stories which gives them a quite*
startling *vividness and persistence* in the memory.

Jung identified dreams as clear messages from the unconscious and regarded intense emotional charges as indications that the unconscious was attempting to communicate with the conscious mind. Persistent or repeated dreams or imaginings were regarded by Jung as very significant communications. To the extent that horror is dream-like, and vivid, therefore, it helps readers do inner work.

The ability to foster inner work is what distinguishes horror from terror. James B. Twitchell (1985) maintains that terror

is external and short-lived; horror is more internal and long lasting. (p. 16)
A generation from now there will be a different "terror in the aisle." But
horror is different. We will keep returning to watch a werewolf transform,
the vampire bite the virgin, Dr. Frankenstein's experiment in the laboratory,
or Dr. Jekyll meet Mr. Hyde, and we will probably continue this interest until
we resolve whatever it is in these myths that is unresolved in ourselves. The
distinction between horror and terror has nothing to do with violence and
grue; it has everything to do with the psychological resonance of sequence
and imagery. (p. 20)

Other commentators articulate benefits that horror can have. Terry Heller (1987) argues that psychoanalytic theory explains how horror can act as a container for dealing with repression by bringing "readers into carefully controlled contact with symbolic representations of the culturally forbidden" (p. 72), often highlighting how culture represses physical pleasure and sexuality.

Philip Hallie (1969) suggests horror can require readers to become both victim and perpetrator, which forces them to rethink and complicate what culture defines as good and evil. Paradox is used to simultaneously produce both empathy and fear, attraction and repulsion. Stephen Neale (1980) is provocative, maintaining that horror is "emancipatory" work insofar as it uses symbols and codes to challenge culture's standards for normality, and clear "black-and-white" definitions and one-sidedness that works against psychic wholeness and integration.

Vinz (1996) argues that the appeal of horror goes beyond the psychology of an individual:

> Horror fiction has been a cultural text for centuries, satisfying a popular impulse to look differently and elsewhere for explanations that transgress the actual world as it is represented or understood . . . Beyond the pure stimulation of physiological responses to fear, the thrill of subversion may explain adolescents' fascination with horror . . . Horror fiction makes gaps in reason visible and, in so doing, opens spaces—those specks of white—where the logic of the world falters and stumbles. (p. 14)

In short, there are compelling reasons why horror has such a broad appeal.

THE PLEASURE OF PLAY

As we've seen, horror provides the possibility for inner work and intellectual pleasure. But, as always, the pleasure readers take from their reading starts with the pleasure of play. Here's a catalog of what the survey respondents said when we asked why they like horror:

- Short, hooks you in right away
- They are fast-paced, pulls you in right away
- Shock value!
- Suspense—cliffhanging
- Creepiness—gives me a thrill
- Vicarious danger, extremeness, fear, adventure
- Feels like war but in a game-like way
- Involves action and emotions—more than any other kind of book
- Forces an emotion—you can't be cool or detached
- Creepiness that is absolutely over the top—it's wild—you don't know what to expect
- Real—but to the extreme—so it captures what being a teen feels like to us

The pleasure of reading horror starts with the thrill, the experience of entering the story world and the emotional investment that entering demands. As was true for the other play pleasures that we've discussed, the horror readers extended this play pleasure by reading sequels. One survey respondent wrote, "What I'm reading is related to other books I like—there tend to be lots of sequels." Another noted, "I like getting to know and follow the characters book by book."

The Pleasure of Work

The pleasure of reading horror may start with thrill, but as one survey respondent explained, it doesn't end there. She wrote that she enjoys horror because of the suspense but noted that its "suspense that stays with you after you've read and haunts you and chills your bones—first makes you feel and then makes you think."

Think about what? Another respondent explained, "There's no horror unless it grabs something inside." A quick catalog provides a clear indication that for readers of horror something inside does indeed get grabbed when they read horror, for their reading allows them to engage in addressing fundamental issues:

- [Horror is] about the dark and darkness and being caught in the darkness. Exploring the darkness without a flashlight!

- [Horror is] about surprise, about what is there that you have ignored or just haven't seen or wanted to see. Then you have to face it.

- [Horror] makes you disgusted. It's about insane things. Things that have gone crazy . . . Then you either run away or deal with it.

- [Horror is about] redoing the normal—going below the surface.

- Horror is kind of relieving because you can see that your life is better.

- [Reading horror] is searching for how to be powerful—how to resist extreme evil or power.

- [Horror] is about very real but unseen forces and it uses monsters and symbols and things to help us see them.

- Gives us coping skills—for scary situations, for the unknown.

- [Horror provides] "What I would do/What if?" practice. We are all going to face scary challenges.

- [Horror shows] things to avoid and that you should be scared of—they are like caution signs.

- Relatable—[horror] relates to the tough things about being a teenager—everything we are experiencing.

One reason that reading horror invites introspection and a critical analysis of significant issues is that reading it provides a liminal space. We've mentioned the notion of liminality several times in this book, but it was so important to our survey respondents that we think it's worth a more extended explanation now. A liminal state is a threshold state, one that's between two other states. For example, when readers enter the story of a narrative, they experience that world as a real place, even though it is not. Our survey respondents may not have been able to define a liminal state, but they surely recognized its power:

- The world is violent. But [horror] gives us a chance to deal with the violence without actually being involved.

- [Horror is about] the worst kind of life-ruining dangers. But it's not happening to you. You get to watch. That's why you can handle it.

- [Horror is about] terrible things that could really happen to you but in some other way.

- [Horror gives you] another world. It might say something about our world but it is not our world. That makes it safe and makes it really fun. And fun to see the connections if you can.

- [Horror] taps into your deepest anxieties and keeps you anxious. Like missing a step on the stairs sort of feeling and you are just suspended in space. It's about the realest of feelings and ideas and things but in an unreal way.

One respondent spun out his response more fully. He noted that, "Horror is anything that directly gets your deepest fears and insecurities." He continued:

I think we are all afraid that we will do something that is out of control that we can't take back that will haunt us forever. We are all afraid that we are not right about really important things and afraid to admit that we do things that are really wrong. Sometimes that makes you act even stronger.

Reading horror allowed readers to try things they would not ever want to really experience and they could try out responses and reactions in a contained and protected liminal space. This liminality allowed them the opportunity to do inner work. And that inner work was sure to be relevant because, as one survey respondent explained, "Junior High is a horror show!"

When we shared our data with Jungian analyst Scott Hyder, he explained the qualities of inner work:

> There are three levels of response 1) the intra-psychic individual response, 2) the interpersonal or social, and 3) the transpersonal, which has to do with our own and humanity's relationship with the spirit and the planet. There's no longer any sense of the divine or the enlightened in our materialistic world, so this lack finds expression through horror texts. And the horror is real, both in our individually lived experience but also collectively and environmentally. Kids are aware of this on some level and need to deal with it. I think this is why they consider the books very real because psychologically they are real and help them deal with real challenges.

He continued:

> I think that books, movies, and art are powerful kinds of containers because what is repressed is given a form and seems somehow outside oneself, though personally resonant. These artworks give expression to our fears but in a container. There's a real value of creating an image and word of what horrifies us. It can give a sense of liberation and even fun. This process gives us a sense of containment and it can be a great relief to name and to experience our anxiety and fear in a container . . . [this fear] can then be more consciously integrated.

The Pleasure of Figuring Things Out

Some of the readers of horror seemed to take a more detached intellectual perspective. Robert, one of the 14 central informants you met in the first part of the book, made a distinction between "slasher" kinds of horror without a "big perspective," which he disparaged, and the horror he liked to read that resembled the distinction Twitchell (1985) made between terror and horror. The horror Robert liked to read:

> . . . give[s] you a perspective of the horror that's within our world in a way. Cuz there's maybe a psycho, it can give you an idea of how messed up people are. And then there are like some horror perspectives that are more into horrific, like something more horrific within nature, kind of, and how our impact on nature can cause bad things and stuff.

John, another of our 14 central informants, also noted that horror let him examine big perspectives because it's about "broken relationships—between people and other people, between groups, between people and nature."

Some survey respondents spoke more generally about the kind of intellectual pleasure reading horror provides:

- You see things differently—you go through a door and everything is different and seen from a new angle.

- It makes you wonder.

- It's psychologically intriguing.

- It's deviant and that's interesting. Where is the line and what happens when you go over it or someone who affects you is over it?

- It explores the forbidden.

- It activates the imagination.

Other readers talked about the particular intellectual pleasures they derived from their favorites. Robert, for example, spoke about *Unwind* and its sequel *Unwholly* by Neil Shustermann, novels whose plots revolve around "retroactive abortions" of teenagers to enable the harvesting of body parts and genes to make futuristic Frankensteins. The books, he said, are about "genetics, abortion, body harvesting—maybe stuff we can do but we don't have the morality to really think through." But his reading allowed him to do so.

Miss Peregrine's Home for Peculiar Children by Ransom Rigg, a book illustrated by vintage photographs, also proved popular. The story opens after a horrific family tragedy sends sixteen-year-old Jacob journeying to a remote island off the coast of Wales, where he discovers the crumbling ruins of the home. Jacob finds that the children housed there were more than peculiar and may still be alive and on the island. One of the respondents noted that, "This book is all about human evil and dealing with evil and what can happen when we think of people as different."

Horror, it seems, encourages and assists students to challenge what Mikhail Bakhtin (1968) called "the routine of life" and claim their right "to be free from all that is official and consecrated" (p. 257). Vinz (1996) explains that the students in her study experienced this freedom. As she puts it, they:

. . . understood the temporary status of the "freedom" they experience through reading. But, temporary status still gives an opportunity to play with, transgress, and oppose . . . Reading horror can be an act of resistance, a playful

manipulation of conventional meanings to see what else might be there, and an exploration of what is kept under tight control or repressed. (p. 16)

WHAT WE CAN LEARN FROM OUR READERS OF HORROR

For these readers, the monsters they encounter, the fear they face, and to some degree, the blood, gore, and violence they experience while reading horror hold a real fascination. Can readers' identities be shaped by the representations in these texts? The survey respondents didn't talk about the social pleasures they derived from their reading of horror, but the myriad examples they provided of the inner work they did and the intellectual pleasure they experienced make us think it's possible—though, not in the simplistic directly causal way that cultural commentators might think.

What does seem certain is that these texts give readers psychic material to work with, and ways to deal, in safe, liminal, contained spaces, with their deepest individual fears as well as with global issues like climate change and collective neuroses like greed and violence.

On an individual level, these texts can allow readers to deal with their various identities, engage with different psychic figures from their personalities, bring out what is feared and repressed so it can be examined, and consider their own emotions, desires, and personal growth challenges through their transactions with characters and events in the stories. Doing this kind of inner work leads to richer inner lives and will certainly have effects on our outer lives as well.

In school, we think it is entirely possible to consciously study the history of horror through folktales. We might consider their psychic uses and current applications, various archetypes and how they play out in popular culture, the costs and benefits of technological progress, and individual and collective neuroses—their effects and how best to address them. Such inquiries would move well beyond the reading of horror books and into other substantive learning, social work, and even volunteer service.

Horror could also provide the occasion to address aspects of the Common Core State Standards that seem to be vexing for teachers of the English language arts. The CCSS call for an increased emphasis both on informational texts and on interdisciplinarity. Imagine an inquiry unit centered on the question, "What scares us and does that change depending on time and place?" To think seriously about that question, students would have to read both classic and modern horror. They would also have to read psychological and anthropological texts. It's clear that this would provide a great opportunity to demonstrate that students should see fiction and nonfiction as complementary in addressing basic human problems.

A thoughtful consideration of horror also can provide the occasion for doing serious work on comparison, extended definition, and classification, three of the nine kinds of informational texts cited by the CCSS. Remember earlier when we cited Twitchell's distinction between horror and terror? Students could take up that distinction in talking and writing about their reading, doing various kinds of comparing and defining.

Or they could develop a classification system for subgenres of horror. Horror author Joanna Parypinski (2011) argues that labeling something as horror "doesn't narrow it down as much as you think" and goes on to delineate 12 subgenres. Students could critically consider her list, and the lists of others, and develop their own. We've written at length elsewhere about activities that would help prepare students to do such writing (Wilhelm, Smith, & Fredricksen, 2012), so we won't go into detail here. Our point is this: A thoughtful examination of horror not only provides students the opportunity to read a very popular genre but also to work toward important academic goals. By accepting our students' interest in horror, we enable them to consider their own fears, anxieties, and emotional charges, and to explore how they might contain and control these—through their own composing and reading. In this way, we're doing our students a lifelong favor—and performing a service to society as well.

CHAPTER 10

Thinking the Unthinkable

Looking for Answers in Dystopian Fiction

Jazzy is Jeff's younger daughter. She's always been a passionate reader. In second grade, she picked up Book One of Lemony Snicket's *A Series of Unfortunate Events* and was hooked. Jeff remembers how she wouldn't come to dinner because she was riveted to the couch reading one of the books, groaning and writhing inside an afghan yelling out, "Oh no! No!" as another unfortunate event occurred. She read every book in the series more than once, and a highlight of her childhood was meeting Daniel Handler, the author behind the alter ego of Lemony Snicket.

She now says that these books were her first brush with dystopian novels, a passion of hers to this day:

> *A Series of Unfortunate Events* has some common [dystopian] themes—kids are in a crappy world they are trying to overcome. There's a "power to the protagonist" thing. It's all about overcoming difficulties—finding the strength and smarts to do that—and although it is so crappy and so hard and so long but you think they can come through—and they do, too. There is something

enticing about saying, "this sucks and it is horrible but these human beings are going to overcome this or die trying and they are going to expose the unfairness." I like seeing what people can go through and overcome. That is just uplifting to me.

WHY DYSTOPIA?

As Jazzy's previous quote suggests, a *dystopia* is a society in which misery and negative conditions prevail due to oppression or abuse at the hands of powerful authorities. Or, a dystopia may be a utopia, in theory only, gained through horrifying sacrifices and catastrophic costs. There are dystopian stories of fallen worlds from time immemorial. In Northrup Frye's (1957) terms, dystopias are worlds of irony, resulting from some kind of tragedy, and requiring a hero to restore them to wholeness and comedy. They come in many varieties, from totalitarian dystopias to cyber-punk dystopias, to tech-noir dystopias, to ecotopian novels—one of Jazzy's favorites because they "look at environmental problems that are screwing us up."

Dystopian stories have a long history. Indeed, the Parsifal story from the legends of King Arthur and the Roundtable is an archetypal dystopian narrative. There are many versions of the Parsifal legend. (Katherine Paterson retells one version in her YA classic *Park's Quest.*)

The story begins when the Fisher King, the visionary Lord of the Grail Castle and surrounding environs, is seriously wounded in the thigh during battle with a pagan knight. His wounds are so severe that he is suspended, in the greatest of pain, between life and death. As is often true in myth and legend, the land of the king mirrors his condition and lies in total desolation.

Each night, the Fisher King presides over his innermost court where the Holy Grail, the chalice from the Last Supper, is kept. The king's agony is worsened because all his court can eat the bread and drink from the Grail except him. He is so close to the healing bread and wine, but cannot partake or be healed until his curse is lifted. Only a hero can heal the king and the land from its dystopian state.

The story shifts to Parsifal, an adolescent, living with his mother in the wilds but eager to leave home and become a knight. Parsifal, whose name means innocent fool, is full of feeling, in contrast to the might and intellectual knowledge of the Fisher King. Parsifal is out playing and sees five knights ride by. He follows the knights to Arthur's court and asks to become a knight. He then discovers a mentor, Gournamond, who trains Parsifal as a knight and instructs him to search for the Holy Grail. He is told to ask "Whom does the Grail serve?" when he sees the Grail.

Parsifal sets out on his quest and vanquishes many knights. He spares them all on the condition that they become knights of the Round Table. Sometime later, Parsifal finds himself lost in the woods, but then he sees a man fishing from a boat on a lake. The man on the boat is the Fisher King engaged in the only activity that brings him relief. The Fisher King tells Parsifal to go down the road a little way and cross the drawbridge to enter the Grail Castle.

Once inside the Grail Castle, Parsifal is bathed, fed, and led to the Grail ceremony. He observes the ceremony and wants to ask Gournamond's question, but does not, heeding a warning his mother had given to not to ask too many questions. Thus he fails in his quest. The Fisher King gives Parsifal a sword and sends him on his way.

Parsifal continues to vanquish many enemies in the dark forests, always seeking the Grail Castle but never again finding it. Parsifal resolves never to sleep in the same place twice until he once again finds the Grail Castle. Many years later he finds himself in a dark wood and is directed once again to where the Grail Castle can be found. When the Grail Procession enters the castle, Parsifal stands and asks "Whom does the Grail serve?" Instantly, a heavenly voice booms: "The Grail serves the Grail King!" lifting the curse. The Fisher King is able to partake of the bread and wine and is healed. His kingdom comes into bloom and all harmony is restored.

Many of the structural features of the Parsifal legend are also present in contemporary dystopian writing: the fallen world, the hero, the innocent, the mentor, the ruler, the struggle and failures, and the eventual righting of the dystopian world. So, too, are many symbols and motifs: quests and questions, thresholds, nature/innocence vs. modernity/technology; light and darkness; blight and ultimate healing.

The enormous success of Suzanne Collins' *The Hunger Games* and its sequels demonstrate the genre's popularity. Other dystopian novels popular amongst the readers in our study were the California trilogies by Kim Stanley Robinson, the Uplift series by David Brin, and *The Carbon Diaries* by Saci Lloyd. Canonical dystopian novels such as *1984, Brave New World,* and *Fahrenheit 451* are often taught in schools as is the YA classic *The Giver.*

The Pleasure of Play

Like Parsifal, Jazzy is full of feeling as she reads. As we've seen throughout this book, the pleasure of play, of entering a story world so fully that readers feel as though they experience it, is the foundation upon which the other pleasures are built. Jazzy put it quite simply: "I just love these books. You get so into them. You can't put them down." And later: "Usually the story [is] about overcoming adversity—who doesn't love a story like that? Because then you read along and get to fight for justice, too." Jazzy almost becomes a character when she reads, so deep is her engagement in the story.

That engagement is always rewarded:

> Ultimately it's exciting because the good usually wins. Hopeful. Morally satisfying. Our culture is dystopian: Politics, governments, all these shootings—some aspects of our culture are really close to dystopia but there are a lot of good people doing good things. I don't like reading the newspaper because it's like "This is depressing!"

Why aren't dystopian novels depressing? Jazzy explained that it's because of the characters. Indeed Jazzy was enormously articulate about the play pleasure she derived from caring about characters:

> In [dystopian fiction] you spotlight someone good. Newspaper highlights the bad. Yeah! It's important to be strong and independent, resistant. . . . The characters [protagonists of dystopias] have a real sense of self in the fact that they have a cause and are fighting for it—they have thought out why they are fighting for this. Their struggle is to be true to themselves and their vision of a better world.

She continued:

> You want somebody to root for and maybe somebody to root against. I was reading this series and the first book was *Insurgent* by Veronica Roth. You are really rooting for the characters in this uprising and you are rooting against the authorities controlling them. Then you find out that this is just a controlled experiment run by people from the outside. Then you are even angrier. What would it be like to know your experience and suffering and struggle wasn't real or necessary and was totally manipulated?

And later:

> These stories give you somebody to root for. Definitely. Because a protagonist is never someone who goes along with things. But she says, "This is messed up. Let's beat this." Of course you want someone to defeat corporations and overcome the authority and toss off whatever wrath and wrap they are under—whatever is keeping them from being themselves. It makes you feel better that other people are resisting, too. It is encouraging, even though it is a story, that people can identify wrongs in government and

society and can find something to do about it. . . . It's also really clear, like a sports game, and you know who to root for.

One of the characters Jazzy rooted for was Katniss from *The Hunger Games*:

It's up to young people to commit the ultimate acts of rebellion and build things for a better future. The older people are in the status quo. That gives me [as a reader] a sense of possibility and power. A lot of times the main character, like Katniss, has to resist while pretending to conform to some degree. She plays the games on her own terms. That's what you have to do as a teenager or young person. You go along and then strike when you can.

She continued:

I really love Katniss. She summarizes it all for me. She really doesn't want to be a hero but when she has to save her sister she automatically signs up. She is a regular person and she refuses to be desensitized and remains true to herself. She's all about independence, strength and not giving in. . . . The books [*The Hunger Games* trilogy] are about real problems: war, famine, power, oppression of the poor and people who think differently, inequality on an unbelievable scale—which I think we have in this world and in our country—so Katniss is facing unbelievable stress but she makes her own way on her own terms—and even in the Games she plays it the way she wants to—being true to herself and not killing out of sport or hate. . . . Really, she doesn't want to be in this position, but once she is, she goes for it in her own way. . . . She does it for her sister, for her District, and for justice.

The intensity of Jazzy's feelings for Katniss and the intensity she takes in the pleasure of play are quite clear.

She wasn't alone. Michelle, one of our 14 central informants, also talked about the pleasure of play in regards to dystopian fiction. You might recall that Michelle had an interest in writing and reading government conspiracy stories. This interest drew her to reading dystopian novels, as such conspiracies are often central to the plot. Michelle noted that dystopias are extrapolations of current trends and predictions about the future: "Like if humankind goes one way, then we'll end up like *The Hunger Games*." She saw such books as cultural and societal critiques, particularly of authority and government, and as calls to be wide-awake and distrustful of the status quo. She found such novels "terribly exciting" because of their connection to reality and the skin she felt that she had in the game.

The Pleasure of Work

The intense experience of play motivated Jazzy's inner work, as she explained to Jeff:

> I usually like female characters but I like some male ones. I like Peeta in *The Hunger Games* because he is true to himself, too, plays by his own rules, and bends some rules to his advantage. He doesn't have the typical strengths that you think would help him, but he uses [what strengths he possesses] to his advantage. . . I relate to the characters but I don't feel like I am them. I usually don't see what I am in them, but what I would like to be. Usually the lead [I like] is a feminist—they're like "I am not going to put up with any crap. You can't tell me what to do." I don't like that [being told what to do] either—I don't know if you knew that about me or not! Resistance. Independence. I guess in many ways I don't see what I am in them [the protagonists], but what I would like to be and what I think I could be if push came to shove.

Jazzy's reading allows her to do the inner work of declaring the kind of person she wants to become. She continued this theme throughout her interview: "The sense I want is: WE can do it! We can make the world better." And later: "If you look at the world today, with all the problems and the problems that are coming, it is certainly going to be up to the younger generation to make things right." And again:

> There's a lot of worry and anxiety, I think, about the future, and these books help you think about the issues we need to be facing and dealing with. Our generation is going to have to make a big shift and we'll have to reform stupid and unjust rules and traditions.

Ultimately she provided a succinct summary of the work dystopian novels let her do:

> Adults sometimes think these books are depressing. But the books are hopeful! That is part of their allure. I don't want to read to get depressed. Or if I get depressed I want it to be in a good way—really thought provoking and make me think, stay in my mind, think about the way I want to be and how I want to be and the way I want the world to be.

Jazzy's quest is reminiscent of Parsifal's, the innocent fool who is required to heal the

Fisher King and his land. Just as Parsifal must undertake quests to ready himself for this healing, Jazzy reads to ready herself.

She went on to spin out a particular example:

> This summer I read *Matched* by Ally Condie where when you turned 16 or 17 you went to this matching ceremony and your significant other was identified for you, done by this computer program that mapped everything out for you—chooses your career and where you would live, your mate.
>
> You didn't get any say—you got assigned this person and there was this complete faith that the government could find your perfect match—no thought. No questioning. Your partner is assigned by a computer and you learn about your person through a microchip and you meet them once and then at an assigned age you marry them and it is the same for every person, mapped out, total control—there is no thought that it doesn't have to be that way. But there is a glitch in the system for the main character—another person's face flashes—who is an unmentionable and you can't be matched with one of them and that is her match.
>
> It made me think so much about how we accept things that could be different all the time. It made me think about what I accept that I could question. That's why you root for the character. Maybe this isn't her fate; maybe she can take a stand and exert some control. And maybe I can exert more control, too. So you are figuring it out with her, but also in parallel for yourself in your own situation, which you have to figure out—it's like a parallel puzzle. How can things be different—and better—for her and for me—if I can apply what the book is teaching to my own life.

As we see, Jazzy enjoys the intellectual pleasure of figuring things out. But her pleasure doesn't stop there as she uses what she figures out to make a better world.

She talks about another favorite book in similar terms:

> [*Legend*] was about how the West Coast and Midwest are at war. The two protagonists—one works for the republic and one is against it. The whole problem is that the republic is lying to the people and making them fight for things under false pretenses and false news. One of the themes is that people are kept in the dark politically and that is disturbing because I think that happens all the time to us—things are hidden from us and others like the politicians and media control what we know so they control what we think and then what we decide and do. The story is a means to think about that and where you are going to get your news and validate your information.

> One girl blindly follows the republic and she believes in all these things and she is being trained for the military and the boy lives on the street and he sees how things really are. She is supposed to be hunting him because he is a con artist. She finds him and he explains to her a little bit about what is happening and how he knows and she starts to question. And I ask whether there are things I should question. Is there evidence I am refusing to see? It is scary to think about being wrong, about not knowing the truth. It moves me to think about it. I try for it to change how I act—I do try to be less judgmental—more open-minded—I know that I don't have all the info.

Jazzy's comments provide a clear sense that her reading helps her struggle from simple to complex consciousness, and expresses a desire for enlightened consciousness, just as Parsifal was moved through his struggles and failures. We see the process again here when she speaks about *Blood Red Road* by Moira Young: "There's one where the world has been dried up due to climate change. I think about that problem all the time and how I can be part of a solution along with my generation."

Once again, the liminal quality of narratives supported this inner work. Here's how Jazzy put it:

> By supporting the character you are supporting their cause and their values and you are taking a stand, too, and that feels good and then you think about how to take that stand in your life and that is very powerful. It's not as messy in a story [as in life]—you know who to root for. . . I definitely want to know the character and admire their values and pull for them and want to help them and therefore want to help people like them in life.

It's clear that Jazzy is doing a lot of inner work through her reading of dystopian novels: She thinks about her own life situation and challenges, reflects on her own current thinking and how it could be transformed, considers injustice and rehearses how to rectify it, and much more. She questions her own shadow, her own lack of awareness, and her collusion with societal habits that may not be healthy or fair for all. She is interested, like Parsifal, in a more just and harmonious world and in taking an active part in establishing that world, in asking the questions that might bring it into being.

The Pleasure of Figuring Things Out

Jazzy also experienced a more detached intellectual pleasure from her reading. One aspect of this intellectual pleasure was overcoming the unique challenges dystopian novels provide:

> My first YA [dystopian] novels were *The Ear, the Eye, and the Arm*, and then *House of the Scorpion* by Nancy Farmer. . . . At first they seemed a little old for me. It took me a while to figure out this was not the world we live in and then I was shocked and asked, "Where are they, why are things this way?" and I remember it being a challenge, and me being curious, and that curiosity—what is this world and why does it work that way—I was interested in understanding that. . . . That's key for me. You need something to figure out about the world and how it got to be this way and what can be done about it or it's not interesting to read. If you know all the answers, it's not interesting. I love the level of unpredictability [in dystopian novels] because the society functions differently from mine—I have to read but also figure out the rules of that society—the more things to figure out—the more interesting.

The intellectual challenge of figuring out the rules was clearly pleasurable for her:

> These [dystopian novels] are the only books that are really challenging for me. I spend time rereading trying to understand—these authors make up their own lingo, words, situations, but they are parallel to us and so it is a puzzle and it is hard to figure out and that is part of the fun.

But the intellectual pleasure of a book has to extend beyond figuring out the puzzle that a new world provides. She explained, "I want to be shocked out of my usual way of thinking." She continued:

> It is important for me to be challenged by ideas. Otherwise it is just a sappy story. I want challenging ideas. I want to think about things over time. I want the story to stay with me.

One way the stories could stay with her is by providing her what she called "fresh eyes":

> What I love about these [technological dystopia] books is that they help you see the world from a new angle and fresh eyes—see our problems and issues and even our habits that we hardly think of in a new way and see where it might be leading. . . You can see how our priorities and values are leading us to this dystopia.

Her fresh eyes led to some powerful thinking:

> You want to know how the society has come to be so bad, so unjust, or just so plain stupid and you want that to be understandable. You see how it could follow from things going on right now. So you want to rebel. You want to change things. . . . It makes you think about this thing that sociologists call "the shifting baseline"—how things change slowly in crazy directions without you noticing.

Here, the intellectual pleasure of figuring the problem out leads directly to the desire to work for change.

Jazzy gave specific examples of some of the ideas her reading led her to grapple with:

> In the series The Uglies by Scott Westerfeld, the big problem is pressure about looks, and these crazy cultural notions about what's beautiful or normal . . . but in every case there is some underlying cause that has to be taken care of.

Jazzy continued to explain that future dystopias often "pay a lot of attention to technology and what it is doing to us and how it can be misused." Technology, or the lack of it, "seems pretty important in almost all dystopian books." There is an exploration of the meaning and ethics of various technologies—who has access, and how technologies are used and abused:

> *The Hunger Games* is really big on exploring how technology is used to oppress people—it's kind of like *1984* that way [in the way people are monitored by technology], and about questioning reality TV, about how technology disconnects us and desensitizes us—which is kind of the opposite of how lots of people like to think about technology—as connecting us and all good.

Jazzy also noted the intellectual pleasure of applying the lessons of the books to our world. She noted that there's also a kind of "horrible fun in asking what if? And projecting trends into the future and thinking what the future will be like if we don't change things." This process produces an intellectual pleasure of figuring things out and of considering and exploring worlds of possibility.

She provided a specific example:

> I like to be made to think about things being different. I like to have my perspective skewed. Like I got this book *Delirium* by Lauren Oliver. They find a cure for love. Take a pill so you don't fall in love. I think that's delicious! How we classify things as healthy or normal or desirable but you could say it's a disease. I love books that are questioning what is or could be.

And another:

> [Dystopian novels] really make me think about technology. I think more and more technology is a form of control, not of freedom. Used by governments, not the people. I think more and more this is happening. My email sends advertisements based on words in my email. My computer remembers my debit card. I read this article in *Time* when we were reading *1984* about Google tracking us. [In *The Immortal Life of Henrietta Lacks*, the author Jennifer] Skloot writes about tissue removal. You sign a waiver that others can use it any way they like. So there are all these tissue samples and no one, not even the donor, has control over it. Your DNA and info and your interests are all out there for others to exploit. Privacy is a big issue that is important to me that [dystopian novels] explore.

Jazzy wasn't alone in talking about the intellectual pleasure she experienced from reading dystopian novels. So, too, did Michelle, who insisted that dystopias were "kind of like a wake-up call, I guess, for us to think." The protagonists—and the readers—must determine the cause of the dystopia, and then figure out how to resist and what compromises to make, or refuse to make:

> It's like don't rely too much on your government. You know, listen to yourself. The government can be pretty whack sometimes as we talked about before with the government conspiracy thing.

Peter, another of our core informants, was a fan of "sci-fi dystopias." He agreed that dystopias are critiques of authority, society, and government, referencing a canonical dystopian novel to make his point:

> *1984*, you can bring that into politics. Also, there is, if you want something [about a] flawed government or something like that read a few of the Douglass Adams [sci-fi] books because they have some politics in it.

Social Pleasures

Although Jazzy didn't talk explicitly about issues of identity, throughout her interview we saw the social pleasure in establishing identity and aligning oneself with like-minded people, of being able to help such people in the future. Jazzy wants to be challenged to think, to understand more, to move towards personal transformation by her reading.

Her family and friends assisted in that movement:

> School doesn't support reading popular dystopias but only classic ones like *1984*, but I'm lucky in that I feel really supported by my parents and friends to read and think about the books I love.

WHAT WE CAN LEARN FROM OUR READERS OF DYSTOPIAN FICTION

When we asked Jazzy how her school and home reading compared, she had this to say:

> I don't think there should be a distinction between school and life reading. Reading should be fun always, and relevant always, and engrossing always. Taking the time to apply it to students' lives and current events is crucial because otherwise it is just reading for school and it is purely busywork and doesn't mean anything. Identifying themes that are problems and issues in life and then reading around those with the kinds of books kids like [is what should be done in school]. I would be more inclined to read nonfiction if it was connected to problems. I read mostly one thing and that is novels but I would be interested in reading things that are connected to the problems and issues in the [dystopian] books I read.

Jazzy's point echoes one we made last chapter: Fiction and non-fiction can be put into meaningful conversation with each other, and in regard to substantive real world and disciplinary problems. Reading dystopian fiction could raise critical issues taken up by philosophers, political scientists, and others. Jazzy gave a specific example:

> [After reading a dystopian novel] you want to know how the society has come to be so bad, so unjust, or just so plain stupid and you want that to be understandable. You see how it could follow from things going on right now. So you want to rebel. You want to change things. . . . It makes you think about this thing that sociologists call "the shifting baseline"—how things change slowly in crazy directions without you noticing.

We think that she is right—we should make sure that the books we require or encourage kids to read will be compelling and interesting to them in their current state of being, and relevant to their growth as specific human beings, and to the world they live in. We also think reading should be for something meaningful and lead towards something significant.

We have long argued for inquiry-oriented instruction organized around problems that are compelling to students (Smith & Wilhelm, 2010; Wilhelm & Novak, 2011; Wilhelm, 2007; Wilhelm, Boas, & Wilhelm, 2009). We've also argued for reading a variety of texts with differing perspectives on a central issue and putting those texts in conversation with each other (Smith & Wilhelm, 2010). It would be easy to provide the option to read dystopian novels in the context of units across the curriculum—civics, history, government, health, environmental studies, etc. Inquiries framed with essential questions about when it is justifiable to revolt against an established government, how best to enact change, the costs and benefits of technology, or of being a rebel immediately come to mind. Throughout the years, our own students have seemed eager to question the status quo, to relate enthusiastically to rebels, to express concern about fairness and social justice, and to discuss how best to achieve both.

To meet the multimedia standards in the CCSS students could watch and/or make movies or trailers of scenes from dystopian novels. They could create multimodal compositions of their own dystopias. They could do drama work where they interview characters from various dystopias or create a dystopia talk show or museum.

There are many classic and more modern dystopian movies (*The Matrix, A Clockwork Orange, Blade Runner* (adapted from *Do Androids Dream of Electric Sheep?* by Philip K. Dick), *Logan's Run, Metropolis, Soylent Green, The Terminator* and its sequels, *12 Monkeys, V for Vendetta, Never Let Me Go, Alex Rider, Children of Men,* etc.) that can be paired with books. Students could be asked to do a movie club (Wilhelm, 2012c) and compare the movie they viewed to a book they have read or a social problem they are studying. Students could also create dystopia criteria checklists and rate each movie according to the list.

But beyond the instructional ideas, what we learned from dystopia readers reminds us of the heroic quest of the human journey—of Parsifal's journey—that we want our students to successfully pursue. Jazzy is calling for us to create curricula where all students are moving beyond the strictly rational into a transpersonal space that connects them to the environment and to all humankind—and gives them a sense of hope and agency in working towards a better future, not just for themselves but for others and the world itself.

The heroic quest is ultimately about asking and answering the great questions of existence and human effort. Education, in this sense, is a sacred endeavor of bringing students' best possible selves into being, equipping them for their own heroic journeys, for facing and meeting the inevitable challenges that all human beings face. Clifford Mayes (2010) writes that

> the Hero's Journey is a symbol. What it symbolizes is the emotional, intellectual, and spiritual growth of the individual as he or she goes beyond the narrow confines of family and immediate environment in order to seek, find, and ultimately act on a new vision of self, society, world and the cosmos. (p. 11)

The dystopia readers seem to be actively constructing what June Singer (1988) calls a personal mythology, a vibrant infrastructure of mythic narratives, images, patterns, and potentials that inform one's life, whether one is conscious of it or not. It seems to us that one of our tasks as teachers is to help students create and bring into awareness the kind of personal mythologies that Jazzy is already creating and using to read, to reflect, and to imaginatively rehearse for her life.

CHAPTER 11

THE HARRY POTTER PHENOMENON

The Power of Imagination

Harry Potter: Half a billion books sold. Translated into more than 70 languages. None of us have seen a reading phenomenon quite like it. The Harry Potter books clearly provide their readers with great pleasure. In Chapter 3, we discussed how many of our participants took pleasure in their reading of fantasy. In this chapter, we'll focus on the pleasure readers derived from the most popular fantasy series ever written.

Jeff's daughter Jazzy, whom you met in the previous chapter, and Michael's daughter Rachel are passionate readers and admirers of the Harry Potter books, published in the United States by Scholastic. As she was growing up, Jazzy regarded Jeff as "cool," in part, because he was a Scholastic author. This meant that on the day a new Harry Potter book was released, Scholastic would overnight the book to Jeff, marked for morning delivery! Sometimes the books would come with the DVDs.

Michael is a more recent addition to the Scholastic family, but he tried to get cool points from Rachel by mentioning that he and J. K. Rowling now share the same publisher. Michael's all-time favorite birthday gift from Rachel is a Ravenclaw tie, which she gave him with the explanation, "Dad, they're the smart ones."

Jazzy and Rachel love Harry Potter. When we asked why, each of our daughters immediately and unreflectively insisted that "I just like it," or "It's entertaining," or "It appeals to me." When pressed for details, both girls responded with, "Dad, I just like it!" or "It's the kind of story I really like," or "Don't ruin it for me. It's just a good book! No more overanalyzing!" Jeff eventually overcame Jazzy's reluctance to discuss and explain her passion for the Harry Potter series; Michael, however, wasn't able to overcome Rachel's reluctance. So once again, Jazzy will serve as our chief informant, this time joined in her interview with Jeff by her good friend Bennie.

Harry Potter is so familiar that we'll depart from our pattern of beginning with an analysis of the genre and will substitute instead our analysis of Jazzy's reluctance to talk, for we believe that this reluctance signifies something important about her relationship with the books. On one occasion, she said, in a wearied tone: "Dad, don't try to explain so much or make me explain so much." When Jeff asked why not, she replied that:

> [Explaining] can close things off. I want to stay open . . . It [reflecting on reading] can bring stuff up. It can bring stuff up that is hard to say, and feelings that you really can't say, and when it [evokes such feelings] then it's good and it stays with you. It's like growing your insides into something new.

Her statement is reminiscent of Walter Benjamin's (1955) famous essay "The Storyteller" in which he rails a bit against the news, the absolute swarm and buzz of information pervading our lives, "shot through with explanation." He believed that stories worked mysteriously, coming through the back door, expressing something certainly useful, generative, and applicable—but that stories achieve their power mysteriously, through deep, irrational, emotional, and somewhat inexplicable processes. Meanings often accrue over time. Like seeds locked in packets far beneath an ancient city or deep in the soil of our souls, stories can suddenly spring to life and exert their power.

In another instance, Jazzy said that explaining a story or her response to it "is like trying to explain a dream. It's too personal and too . . . just *crazy*!" At another time: "I just want to enjoy [the story] and then sit with the enjoyment for a while!"

Despite this desire to stay on the surface, the connection of stories like Harry Potter to dreams and dreaming was articulated several times by the informants for this chapter. And, as we've explained on several occasions, this connection evokes depth psychology, which relies so much on dreams and dream interpretation, and on imaginative response as the gateway to inner work.

Freud's (1900) *The Interpretation of Dreams* catapulted him into international fame and ushered in a revolutionary era of psychological research and theory. Freud claimed that dreams were the "royal road to the unconscious." For Jung, though, the symbols Freud described were too literal and too "shot through with explanation" as Benjamin might put it. According to McEwan (2012):

In the course of Freud's analysis, the mystery and poetry of dreams—their sheer surprising gift—was almost entirely destroyed. Jung's attitude was very different. For Jung, there was little difference between dreams and poetic art: both worked through imagery and symbol, and it was the task of the analyst to recognize this, without forcing a translation into socially acceptable terms. He felt it was his task to help the dreamer "to honor the forgotten language of himself," asking of any particular dream, "What does it want? For what conscious attitude does it compensate?" This was not the same, he emphasized, as asking, "What does it mean?" (p. 253)

Sometimes Jazzy would resist explaining because "It's too personal," and she often expressed a sense of intense emotional charge. "Reading can make me sad, upset, nervous, but in the end it always makes me feel bigger and also kind of happier in some way." Perhaps this is because the story compensates her, makes her feel more whole, or honors something about her self—even of her shadow—and way of being, or of trying to be, just as Dewey explained pleasure in terms of the subject's identity and growth.

Compensation, according to Jung, is the capacity of the unconscious to influence consciousness. In "The Importance of the Unconscious in Psychopathology" (1914), he introduced the idea, maintaining that the unconscious was intelligent and that

the principal function of the unconscious is to effect a compensation and to produce a balance. All extreme conscious tendencies are softened and toned down through a counter-impulse in the unconscious. (par. 449)

Compensation moves us towards the Jungian goal of wholeness and integration of our total personality.

THE PLEASURE OF PLAY

Jazzy has made a joke of Jeff's push to always interpret what a book or movie means. "You know, Dad, not everything is symbolic!" To which Jeff responds: "Oh, yes it is!" Jazzy often pre-empts one of Jeff's favorite quotes from Charles Sanders Pierce: "I know, I know, the world is a profusion of signs!" And then rolls her eyes.

Jazzy rolls her eyes because, as we've seen throughout the book, she, like the other readers we studied, emphasizes the enjoyable experience of reading rather than anything she took away from the reading—anything exportable and usable, either functionally or psychically.

The pleasure of Jazzy's play was clear:

> This [reading Harry Potter] is so beyond books. There is something magical happening. A turning on of the turned-off imaginations. Like people can pretend they play Quidditch and it is okay. Because it is associated with HP it is okay. I mean there is a Quidditch club at school and people dress up and play it and do all these different scenarios and no one thinks they are weird. I love it when books can give you permission to imagine—I mean school and life cuts off imagination in so many ways, just cuts it off so it is so cool when something turns it on.

The Harry Potter series turned on Jazzy's imagination, so she could enter the story world, and when she did so, she encountered memorable characters with whom she developed a real relationship. She explained:

> I got really attached to the characters—felt like I grew up with them and experienced what they were experiencing—I mean in their lives and also in parallel to my own. It's about characters having problems, going bad in some ways, and then getting better through their own effort and also the help of others and from being in certain situations—isn't that what life is all about?

She continued:

> I really liked the story—the magical world that we don't know how it functions but you get to be part of that—there is mystery but a promise of figuring it out, and you get to root for the people. Being the same age and you can grow up with them. It's a cool world and people to root for and be excited for. They have challenges—little ones but also a really big one—and you want to help them meet that.

She was a special fan of Ron Weasley and his family:

> I wanted to be part of a House and be with these brave people in Gryffindor and eating dinner in the Great Hall and with people coming together in community and fighting *together* for good. And the Weasleys, what a great

family! I mean the Weasleys are so *themselves*. They aren't high class in the terms of that world or even of the book—lots of people [characters] look down on them—but they are so high class! They are about friendship and family and being conscious of your values and good humor under stress and fighting for good and being courageous—getting done what you just have to do.

Bennie embraced Hermione Granger:

I always related most to Hermione—I mean, I was and still am *that* kid—really studious and a rule-follower and proving myself but she was also funny and a good friend and what I want to be. I learned from her how to be more than studious. About elements of friendship and courage and standing up for friends and working through things and maybe even when you have to bend or break the rules.

We'll soon be talking about the inner work the characters helped our readers do, but for now it's important to note how fully and deeply our readers entered their lives.

Kylie, one of our central informants in the romance chapter, was also a Harry Potter fan. She explained the extent to which Rowling's story world came alive for her as a reader:

I absolutely feel that the characters are real. Last summer Harry Potter was ending and I was so invested in it. I had to step back and say "Hogwarts isn't real" and it kind of broke my heart. I like to think that people this cool and dynamic are populating my world. I've grown to love these characters and I want to believe they exist and have good endings or if they are not so good that they have not so happy endings. Here's the funny thing—I think people like them do exist or their characters exist in some ways as part of the personality of certain people. You can even recognize it in them.

Kylie was so interested in the characters' existence that she acts them out to keep them alive:

I do try to see movie companions to books. If I get invested in a series, like Harry Potter, especially, I just have to see the movies. I made a wand, I bought a Hufflepuff tie at Goodwill which I have downstairs. If it's going on for me [with a book], I try to collect stuff. I dress up for movie premieres. It identifies you but even more it helps you immerse yourself even more in the book and bring the unreal of the books into the real realm so you can enjoy it.

Bennie and her brother also brought the books to life through drama. Several times during the interviews, Bennie described acting out specific scenes and inventing new scenes for the books with her brother: "[The scenes were] kind of like fanfics, but we play acted them out [instead of writing them]."

Interestingly, fanfics seem totally in line with a psychological technique extensively developed by Jung called *active imagination*. Active imagination is simply recognizing the images and figures that come up in dreams or imaginative experiences (like reading)—that seem significant, stay with us, or provide an emotional charge—and then dialoguing with these figures and images. The ego-consciousness enters into the unconscious through the imaginative figures and images and is able to converse, in snippets, but sometimes at length, with the unconscious. This can reveal more articulately and thoroughly what the image or figure was trying to communicate through the unconscious. As Johnson (1986) explains:

> *It is this* conscious *participation with the imaginal event that transforms [the process] from passive fantasy to active imagination. The coming together of conscious mind and unconscious mind on the ground of the imaginal plane gives us the opportunity to break down some of the barriers that separate the ego from the unconscious, to set up a genuine flow of communication, to resolve some of our neurotic conflicts from the unconscious, and thus to learn more about who we are as individuals. (p. 25)*

Fanfics and acting out scenes are obviously a kind of immediate pleasure, but they can also provide the foundation for inner work, as we'll soon see.

It's not just the relating to the characters that brings the pleasure of play. Jazzy and Bennie also took pleasure from the humor. Here's Jazzy:

> I liked Books 3 and 4 the best. Three because Sirius was there. It made me happy that Harry had someone in his life that was fighting for him and supporting him— that he had an actual family member. Everything was against him. He learned a lot more about that world of magic and that's when the Marauders' map came— that was the coolest thing ever. That trickery, that feistiness, jokesterness, I loved that so much. I loved that map. I love how it insults people.

And Bennie:

> You can transfigure things and apparate and break rules and that is so exciting. There are all these jokes and gags throughout the books and inside humor and it's funny.

The Pleasure of Work

We've seen how the girls experienced the playful pleasure of entering the story world. That experience in that story world also allowed them to do significant inner work. Here's Bennie:

> I read them from when I was eight years old. I read them through high school. I experienced each of the books differently because I was getting older and the characters were getting older with me and the problems kept getting more serious. [The books] were like guides for growing up or for your life or something like that.

She elaborated:

> [Reading the Harry Potter books] defined my childhood and it will always have this really important place to me in my personality and development. Particularly the lessons of courage and friendship. The lesson that you have to be brave and direct in facing problems—head on. [The books] don't knock you over the head with [that lesson]—it's respectful of me and I think the books are right. [The lessons] are not necessarily directly expressed but it influences me and helps me.

Bennie noted that the magic of the fantasy world was compelling, but she explained that something more was at work as well:

> We all want to be able to fly and be a hero and have magic and have supportive friends like that. In one way, it's all imagination, but in another, it makes you receptive to the magic in your own life and says *pay attention*! And asks you how you can make that kind of experience in your own life.

She continued:

> We [Bennie and her brother Sam] had so many games of make believe about Harry Potter and it was all about dealing with dilemmas and problems like we were facing right then and how to be good friends. We'd sometimes play Quidditch, too, but that was more for just plain fun.

"Plain fun" didn't teach Bennie and Sam about the kind of people they wanted to become. But the books certainly did:

It's not like I'm always thinking "I'm going to be a good friend like Ron Weasley," but it sticks with you somewhere—It's almost like sometimes like you say WWHD: What would Harry or Hermione do or Ron do? But really you are asking what you think is the right thing to do but you are using the characters to help you think about that, to consider that.

Remember when we talked about how dreams help one do inner work? Bennie hadn't read Jung, but she sounds like she has:

Reading is kind of a way and a place to be slow. Going slow helps you get centered. If I am kind of confused I like to take a deep breath and read a book that I like. Like the Potter books are very consoling to return to . . . . reading is kind of consciously and slowly living inside a dream . . . . I think dreams tell you what to remember. You figure out what to remember from a book, too. When you read a great book like the Harry Potter books you feel sometimes like you are remembering something from a dream—something that is really important to you that you almost forgot. Stories can be a bridge between your life and your self, your dreams, ideals, big stuff.

Her reading and rereading helped her tackle the big stuff, as she explained:

There were so many parallels between the characters and myself—but in completely different worlds. [The characters] were relatable, I could see their flaws. I liked that they were not perfect and that helped me see my own flaws and be OK with them, and think I could deal with them.

Jazzy was explicit in her thinking that the books helped her do inner work:

I want to think about being a great friend or being courageous but I also want to think about what things threaten me and keep me from being who I could be. So it's practical but it's also psychological.

So, too, was Kylie:

Harry Potter stands for good triumphing over evil, fighting for good, for imagination, for making choices instead of having others choose for you, for determining what happens in your life. And that a normal person can make a difference. Save the day. Harry is an orphan. He overcame his stepparents. Even Dudley in the end—he pushed back and was really a Muggle villain but in the end he reaches out to Harry. People can change, can make up for things. You can be screwed up and out of control and turn out okay. It is about acceptance of your self. I hated Snape so much but then you find out he is okay despite his wrongdoing and Harry had a reconciliation by naming his kid after him.

All three girls clearly saw their reading of Harry Potter as contributing to their growth. The books helped all three girls become their best possible selves.

The Pleasure of Figuring Things Out

The girls also clearly experienced the pleasure of figuring things out, though that pleasure was informed by the playful pleasure they experienced in entering the story world and the pleasure they took from using the books to do inner work. They were so engaged in talking about that pleasure that Jeff couldn't get a word in edgewise:

BENNIE: *I was really satisfied how some loose ends were tied up but there was still some mystery. It was all really inspiring to me, particularly Harry going back. . . . I still love to re-read them. I have a friend who likes classics and she did her senior project on mythological elements in Harry Potter. She gave a great presentation on the different mythologies and the names and that was really interesting to me—it gave me a different way to think about the books. . . . they were such fun books. I wanted so much to go to Hogwarts and play Quidditch. But they are very human stories, too, and not just like about a dark wizard is trying to kill me. But there are always things that keep you from being good or human or whatever.*

JAZZY: *Don't we all have something to overcome? You always relate the story to things it's not related to. At least I do. I see those kinds of connections. That is how you understand—by relating characters and events and even places to your life. There are practical things like about friendship or bravery but there are mysterious things in the books, too, like there is always a chamber of secrets—things like that.*

BENNIE: *When Hermione and Ron decided to go with Harry to find the horcruxes, that was huge to me; moving and inspiring. That* *you are not isolated in the world—that your life is connected to others. And you can change your life for others or to support others.*

JAZZY: *Sirius being there for Harry. Anytime the Malfoys got involved I got super pissed off. How Dobby was mistreated—so unfair. He was not evil. It was just so unfair. Here are these supposedly "model" people and they have privileges and they are just turd buckets. When Lucius Malfoy or Dolores Umbridge was in a scene—OMG—I just . . . just . . . I'd get so upset!*

BENNIE: *When she [Dolores Umbridge] was making Harry write the lines about lying and she is torturing him. That was the worst. I was just beside myself.*

JAZZY: *The utter inequity and unfairness of it. Here is this really cool wizarding world and Umbridge comes in and ruins it—that is just evil—she mistreats the kids but worse, she ruins the world!*

BENNIE: *When Ginny got taken into the Chamber of Secrets in book 2, at the same time, you found out that she'd been letting the Basilisk serpent loose. She was possessed by Tom Riddle cuz one of his horcruxes was in the book. It wasn't her—she was being controlled. That was so creepy that he was using her for his advantage. It made me think of human beings who are parasites, who use other people. It made me so mad and uncomfortable. The brother-sister aspect (Ron and Ginny) really struck me with Ginny being in such danger and so misused. My brother is two years older than me. I thought about how devastating that would be in real life if your brother or sister was being mistreated and it was beyond your control.*

Think back on Jazzy and Bennie's exchange as you read the CCSS Reading Anchor Standards delineation of the three critical abilities the readers must have. They must be able to:

1. Read closely to determine what the text says explicitly and to make logical inferences from it; cite specific textual evidence when writing or speaking to support conclusions drawn from the text.

2. Determine central ideas or themes of a text and analyze their development; summarize the key supporting details and ideas.

3. Analyze how and why individuals, events, and ideas develop and interact over the course of a text.

Jazzy and Bennie demonstrated all three abilities in spades. Why? We'd argue that their intense involvement in the story world led them to make logical inferences, especially about the characters, much as they do in their own lives, and the thematic generalizations that they made were informed by and contributed to the inner work they were doing.

The girls also derived an intellectual pleasure solving the puzzles they thought the books posed:

JAZZY: *Now that we have all seven books, going back and reading them, you can go back and get some new "a-has," now you see connections and details and get reminded and you see the development and the plan. Things align. There are clues dropped and you can put them together. Like the diary and releasing Ginny, but in sixth book you found out he destroyed a horcrux so that is so cool to see the connections. Namedropping like "Regulus Black" and it becomes relevant again in the seventh book.*

BENNIE: *It was a thrill to pay attention and to put the puzzle together. You get something extra if you pay attention and read critically. There are different levels and I liked doing the deeper level.*

JAZZY: *I liked feeling smart and figuring things out.*

BENNIE: *I liked to figure out the secret of opening the snitch and how that all connected to other things in the stories.*

Social Pleasures

Perhaps more than any of the many books, series, and genres that we've discussed, Harry Potter provided its readers distinct social pleasures.

The Pleasure of Connecting with Family

Both girls talked about how their reading of Harry Potter provided connections to their families. Here's Jazzy:

> [Reading Harry Potter was a] family event. Mom read aloud. All of us sitting down on the couch or reading in bed together. There's definitely a nostalgia element that enhances how I think about reading Harry Potter.

And here's Bennie:

> My brother and I read them together. Then we got the audiotapes [to reread them] and would sit and listen to them together. I would draw when I listened. There was definitely a family aspect of the enjoyment.

The Pleasure of Being One of Many

At several different times, the girls expressed social pleasure in generational terms. Jazzy explained:

> I'm part of a cultural club that grew up with Harry Potter. It gave me a sense of belonging. I loved wondering what I thought was going to happen. Talking to my friends about that. Aligning myself with characters. Waiting so impatiently for the next book. No other group of kids will have that experience again. It kind of marks you as when you grew up and bonds you with other people your age.

She continued:

> Who doesn't know about Harry Potter? It is common ground to relate to, you can crack a Harry Potter joke and people will laugh. It was a shared experience of my generation. It will be true throughout my life with people my age. . . . It's not just your own experience—it's social and cultural. Talking about them—it's a shared experience with all the other people who have read and loved Harry Potter.

Bennie made a similar comment:

> I think each generation has their own Harry Potter. For my parents it was *Lord of the Rings*. I think each generation has their books that help them. Books that encourage imagination. Books that help you with the challenges you are facing. You relate to the characters and are moved by them and it's both conscious and unconscious.

WHAT WE CAN LEARN FROM OUR READERS OF HARRY POTTER

When asked what advice they would give to teachers, Bennie responded:

Teachers should read these books. If you can grab kids with what already excites them, then you are on the way. I never understood why school picks the books that they do except that they are important—but they are not as relatable to us. And as a direct result, kids weren't into it and it was all like pulling teeth. Start with what kids are already excited about. You can teach the same lessons and build the same skills and have more willing participants.

Jazzy didn't exactly agree, though she also saw a place for Harry Potter in schools:

I am not sure I would have had the same experience if the teacher said "read two chapters of Harry Potter" that might have ruined it. But a paired text study of *The Hunger Games* and *Lord of the Flies*, that would really work. You have to encourage people to keep reading what appeals to them. If you pair them with something you want them to read then you have something to build from and relate to. Why would you not do that? If it is age appropriate, why not?

Once again, the girls explored this idea together:

BENNIE: *I mean, I think teachers should ask: What are you trying to teach and get out of a book? And what books will most help that to happen?*

JAZZY: *By not teaching books like bestsellers, teachers start to separate between trashy reading and good literature and it is snobby and actually takes people away from reading and that defeats the point of reading—you want to talk about books you love and if you are embarrassed—[because school is] not giving value to these books—is dismissing the books but also the people reading them. . . . these books were not trashy to me. They were just what I needed. They fed me.*

Jazzy and Bennie make us think that we need to give up or at least think in more nuanced ways about the distinctions we so breezily make between the kinds of texts that should be taught in school and those that shouldn't. In doing that nuanced thinking, what we should keep in mind is the distinction between reading and not reading. When Jeff asked the girls to compare Harry Potter to reading he knew they had been assigned in school, he was surprised to find that they had not completed some of those assigned readings. Bennie, we learned, described herself as "a rule follower," yet she said:

> There are a lot of ways to be successful in classes, particularly English, without doing the reading. School reading is what you are supposed to do. Your own reading is what you want and need to do.

Maybe we can make school reading different. Maybe if we recognize and applaud the pleasures readers take from texts like the Harry Potter series, school reading can be something that students want to do as well.

CHAPTER 12

WHERE DO WE GO FROM HERE?

Our purpose in this book has been to explore the nature and variety of the pleasures that adolescents take from the reading they do outside school. We hope that you're as impressed as we are by the passion and insight of our informants' comments. We hope also that the distinctions we've made among play, work, intellectual, and social pleasures have expanded your understanding of the variety of reading pleasures and that our discussions of the intensity, duration, and timing of those pleasures have provided useful insights into the nature of those pleasures. We hope we have helped you see how these pleasures play out in particular ways in particular genres. In closing, we want to highlight the major instructional principles we've derived from our research in the hope that they are generative in your examination of your practice.

PRINCIPLE 1: MAKE PLEASURE MORE CENTRAL TO OUR PRACTICE

Two stories to start: Jeff and Peggy homeschooled their daughter Fiona for one year, in large measure because Fiona found the work she was asked to do in school so tedious. Jeff and Peggy asked Fiona to choose an area of inquiry she wanted to pursue. She chose to study the Vikings, so Jeff and Peggy began working with her to assemble the materials she could use to learn about them. Much to their surprise, Fiona didn't display any more interest in those materials than she had in the materials she had been given in school. When Jeff asked why, she sighed and said, "Dad, I'm just not interested in Vikings." Jeff was incredulous: "But you chose the topic, Fiona. Why didn't you choose something you are interested in? We gave you the choice!" "Well, I didn't think you really meant it," she responded. So deeply ingrained was the notion that schools make kids do boring stuff that Fiona thought she had to choose boring stuff to do or else it wouldn't really be school.

Why might she have such a belief? When Michael's daughter Rachel was a senior in high school he went to back-to-school night, after swearing—as she made him do every year—that he wouldn't say anything to challenge any of her teachers. Of course, he was always especially interested in her English class. The handout he received in that class listed the texts for the year: *Oedipus*, *Beowolf*, *The Canterbury Tales*, and three Shakespeare plays. In explaining the curriculum, the teacher said, "Well, since we know that students are going to hate all of the readings, we show a lot of films." Yikes!

Remember back in Chapter 2 when we talked about Friedman's definition of the good life for the one who lives it? Such lives can be measured by the intrinsic attitudinal pleasure a person experiences minus the intrinsic pain he or she experiences. What if we resolved to make a major goal of every class to enhance our students' reading lives, to provide immediate and intrinsic pleasure in the reading our students do in school?

We think that the implications of this resolution are enormous. One implication is that we would have to be mindful of the variety of pleasures that readers can take from their reading and not privilege intellectual pleasures, the characteristic province of school. To be sure, throughout this book we've seen examples of our participants taking pleasure in making thematic generalizations, in figuring out metaphors, in carefully analyzing the aesthetic choices an author makes, in making subtle distinctions among related genres, intellectual pleasures all. But we've also seen examples of the pleasure of entering a story world and living through a character's actions, of trying on a character's perspectives and thinking about what it might mean for how one wants to live, of sharing one's reading with friends. We should also choose texts that provide this variety of pleasure (or let our students choose them). And we should expand on and explore pleasures like these through the use of action and drama strategies in response to reading (Wilhelm, 2012b).

Another implication would be to work to expand the range of texts in which students can take pleasure, taking care as we do so to teach in a way that engages students in experiencing the pleasure of texts that they might not select on their own, while recognizing that this pleasure might not be easily forthcoming. Let's think about what our resolution might say about selecting texts. Student choice (Fiona notwithstanding) is safer than teacher choice. Variety is safer than similarity. Think about how different Rachel's class would have looked had students been invited to choose which of the three Shakespeare's plays they'd read. Imagine if they could also choose a YA novel or a contemporary nonfiction text that addresses the issues showcased in the play they chose. Consider the difference if these plays were surrounded not only by films and a self-selected novel, but also by stories, essays, graphic novels, cartoons, and so on that related to the same themes and ideas under discussion. Finally, imagine the students' engagement if the course were built on six units of study rather than six texts. In Chapter 4, we talked about the power of inquiry units framed around essential questions to provide the pleasure of doing inner work. We've written about this idea at length elsewhere (Wilhelm, 2007; Smith & Wilhelm, 2010) so we won't belabor the point here. But we've come to understand that the power of inquiry units resides in part in the pleasures the units provide as well as the reading pain they help students avoid.

As our thought experiment illustrates, we are not calling for eliminating the study of classic or challenging contemporary literature. Indeed, our respondents talked on occasion about how they took pleasure from such texts. Remember Robert's affection for *Les Miserables* and Callie's reading of ee cummings? As we'll explain more fully later in this chapter, we are calling for embedding the teaching of those texts in contexts that foster the pleasure students can take from them.

PRINCIPLE 2: Make Interpretive Complexity Equal to Text Complexity in Planning

We realize that we could be seen to be running afoul of the Common Core State Standards on text complexity in our discussion of Principle 1, but we don't think we are. We're not saying that kids shouldn't read hard texts. Remember the pride Peter took in reading Dumas? We are saying that we should be mindful both of their potential pleasure and their potential pain when we select texts. But we think also that our readers clearly demonstrated the results of enormously complex interpretive work in their comments on texts that wouldn't be regarded as complex in and of themselves.

We think that our data make it clear that we're not dumbing down the curriculum if our students are reading graphic novels, or dark fiction, or Harry Potter. All of these texts require sophisticated strategies for entering a story world. As we've seen, all of them foster inner work built on making thematic generalizations. All of them provide the pleasure of figuring out complicated puzzles and wrestling with big ideas. All of them are consistent with the notion of complexity that Rabinowitz and Bancroft (in press) describe, a notion they contrast to the vision of the Common Core:

> To develop increasing sophistication on the part of students, any pedagogical model needs some kind of roadmap, some kind of trajectory. For us, the ideal literary education would be Euclidean. When we say that, we're not suggesting that education should be inflexible. . . . Rather, we are proposing Euclid as a model because we believe that literary education should begin with the fewest possible number of initial assumptions, and that more complicated interpretations, in later years, should come from increased development and subtler manipulation of those assumptions, rather than from introducing entirely new concepts. Note the difference from the position taken by David Coleman, who has become one of the most prominent and articulate promoters of the Common Core. In "Bringing the Common Core to Life," Coleman argues that "The real distinction in the growth of reading is of course the level of complexity of the text that you're managing" (10) (emphasis added). Of course, Coleman's "of course" is intended to brush aside objections before they are raised, but we'll raise ours anyway. For us, what's significant is not the complexity of the text, but the complexity of the interpretive act you're performing.

We think that students ought to experience the pleasure of both kinds of complexity—of texts and of interpretations. If familiar texts and YA novels allow for greater interpretive complexity—due to their familiarity or how closely they address student interests—then that is enough reason to include them in the curriculum.

PRINCIPLE 3: ENACT THE THREE CS

A cryptic heading, we know. But before we explain it, we'd like to share the educational theorist from whom it was derived: Father Guido Sarducci, once a regular contributor to *Saturday Night Live*. You might remember (or might have seen on reruns) Father Sarducci, a representative of the Vatican as played by comedian Don Novello. Our favorite of his routines and the one that has influenced us the most was his proposal for a Five Minute University. His idea was simple: If you would just teach students what they would remember five years after the course was over, college could be over in five minutes. Spanish I, for example, would be "¿Cómo está usted?" and then you'd be done. Pretty funny. But pretty challenging, too. What it means for us as teachers is that we have to build our lessons, units, and courses around skills and ideas that students will continuously use and hence remember and transfer. What it means for us as writers is that we have to realize that as much as we'd like you to remember every detail of all of our data and every nuance of all of our arguments, you won't. But we do hope that you remember how our data and our arguments have supported three key approaches to instruction. And to help you remember, we present them as the three Cs.

C1: The Chance to Talk

The two of us met when Jeff was Michael's student at the University of Wisconsin. Jeff explained to Michael that he planned to use symbolic story representations as a primary source of data for his dissertation. In brief, in symbolic story representations, students are first asked to select a scene in their reading that they found especially compelling and then to visually represent the setting of that scene in some way. They then have to populate the setting with cutouts that symbolize the characters in the scene, the relationships among the characters, themselves as readers, and the strategies they employed, and then talk about the scene and how they read it. Michael was adamant, "Nope. It won't work," he said. "They won't be able to talk about something so complex." Jeff responded, "Let's wait and see." When he brought in videotapes of his students doing the symbolic story representations and the extraordinary data they generated through this method (which he reports in *You Gotta BE the Book,* 2008), Michael was amazed.

Since that time, Michael has been a convert and both of us have been encouraging teachers to tap the expertise of their students by making students' talk about their reading absolutely central in their classes. Despite that commitment, we were astonished at how amazingly articulate our readers in this study were about their reading when we simply asked them to talk about it. We learned so much about what, how, and why kids read from them. You know the old adage, "By your students you'll get taught?" You will, if you let them.

How you let them is up to you, of course. In the sections that close each chapter we've talked about a variety of discussion and drama techniques to get students talking. What's important is not so much how you do it, but that you do it. Moreover, we want to stress that we learned from every single kid in this study. Some of them were very successful in school, but most of them were not. In fact, some were close to failing. Others had identified disabilities. But when they talked, they said some extraordinary things. And as our analyses of social pleasures clearly reveals, if we give them the chance, they can teach each other. Our readers hungered for the chance to connect through books and to experience other perspectives.

We recognize that teachers have expertise that students don't. The bulk of our professional writing has centered on our ideas for how to help students develop that same expertise through teacher modeling and mentoring. However, we are saying that our students do have surprisingly sophisticated insights into their reading—insights that can be crucially important instructional resources if we only we invite our students to share.

C2: Choice

How can we know what texts will bring our students the most pleasure? Well, we can't. Remember Callie and her talk about dark fiction:

So if I were responding to a situation in a fiction state of mind, I would probably be like the teen heroine in this fiction state of mind where something horrible happens to them, but then they emotionally grow and strive above it. That's my fiction voice. But a more realistic dark character, something really horrible happens and I have no idea what to do and I think and I ponder about what the possibilities are as I try and try desperately to overcome this situation but never really do and end up moving on with this situation that still is left hanging. Because that's a way more realistic way of life.

Now contrast that with Kylie's comment about romances:

The [heroine] has to make things clear to her love, and usually has to organize things . . . for them to be together which she has to do one step at a time because usually things are pretty complicated! And then they have to really see and really care about each other—hopefully forever. HEA [Happily Ever After], baby!

What book is going to appeal to both girls? Hmm. If we're committed to maximizing our students' textual pleasure, and if we can't know what books our students are going to take pleasure in, we have to let them choose, at least on occasion.

C3: Create a Context that Supports Pleasure

We've argued throughout the book that inquiry units built around essential questions supports students' reading pleasure. Why? They provide a context in which students can read a wide variety of texts. They allow for conversations to happen across texts, which means that people who read different texts still have something to talk about together.

Other contexts make pleasure less central. Think about an American literature class that's arranged chronologically. We know we just wrote that we can't predict the texts in which students will take pleasure, but we're willing to bet that modern texts will appeal to more readers than older ones.

Sometimes, contexts privilege one pleasure at the expense of others. Spending weeks and weeks doing a close reading of a text privileges intellectual pleasure at the expense of play pleasure. As we noted in our own stories, the intellectual pleasure close reading can provide is something to be reckoned with. We want our students to experience it. But we want them to know that reading provides other kinds of pleasures as well.

We want to be the kind of teachers who help our students fall in love with books in ways that foster a lifelong devotion to reading. If we are to succeed, then we need to keep—at the forefront of our attention and in all of its various forms—the rich, complex, and profound pleasures of reading.

REFERENCES

Applebee, A. N., Langer, J. A., Nystrand, M. & Gamoran, A. (2003). Discussion-based approaches to developing understanding: Classroom instruction and student performance in middle and high school English." *American Educational Research Journal* 40: 685–730.

Appleman, D. (2010). *Critical encounters with literature*. New York: Teachers College Press.

Bakhtin, M. (1968). *Rabelais and his world*. (H. Iswolsky, Trans.). Cambridge, MA: Harvard University Press.

Barthes, R. (1975). *The pleasure of the text* (R. Miller, Trans.). New York: Hill and Wang.

Beach, M. (2011, Dec. 6). *Can romance novels teach you everything you need to know about love?* Retrieved from http://shine.yahoo.com/love-sex/romance-novels-teach-everything-know-love-173100387.html.

Beaudet, D. (1990). *Encountering the monster: Pathways in children's dreams*. Berkeley, CA: University of California.

Benjamin, W. (1955). The Storyteller. In D. J. Hale, (Ed.), *The novel: An anthology of criticism and theory 1900–2000* (pp. 361–378). Malden, MA: Blackwell Publishing.

Bereiter, C. (2004). Reflections on depth. In K. Leithwood, P. Mcadie, N. Bascia & A. Rodriguez (Eds.), *Teaching for deep understanding* (pp. 8–12). Toronto: EFTO.

Booth, W. (1983). A new strategy for establishing a truly democratic criticism. *Daedalus, 112*, 193–214.

Booth, W. (1988). *The company we keep*. Berkeley, CA: University of California Press.

Brown, S. (2009). *Play: How it shapes the brain, opens the imagination, and invigorates the soul*. New York: Avery.

Bruner, J. (1986). *Actual minds, possible worlds*. Cambridge, MA: Harvard University Press.

Carter, M. (Ed.). (1988). *Dracula: The vampire and the critics*. Ann Arbor, MI: UMI Research Press.

Clark, C. & Rumbold, K. (2006). *Reading for pleasure: A research review.* London: National Literacy Trust. Retrieved from www.literacytrust.org.uk/research/Reading%20 for%20pleasure.pdf

Coles, R. (1989). *The call of stories: Teaching and the moral imagination*. Boston: Houghton Mifflin.

Connolly, W., & Smith, M. W. (2003). Dropping in a mouse: Reading poetry with our students. *The Clearing House, 76*, 235-240.

Csikszentmihalyi, M. (1990). *Flow: The psychology of optimal experience.* New York: Harper & Row.

Currie, G. (2013, June 1). Does great literature make us better. *New York Times.* Retrieved from http://opinionator.blogs.nytimes.com/2013/06/01/does-great-literature-make-us-better/?_r=0.

Damasio, A. (2005). *Descartes' error.* New York: Penguin.

Damasio, A (2010). *The brain that changes itself.* New York: Penguin.

Dewey, J. (1913). *Interest and effort in education.* Boston: Houghton Mifflin and Cambridge, MA: The Riverside Press.

Dewey, J. (1916). *Democracy and education.* New York: The Free Press.

Diamond, J. (1999). *Guns, germs, and steel: The fates of human societies.* New York: W. W. Norton.

Dissanayake, E. (1988). *What is art for?* Seattle, WA: University of Washington Press.

Dissanayake, E. (1992). *Homo aestheticus: Where art comes from and why.* Seattle, WA: University of Washington Press.

Erikson, E. (1963). *Childhood and society* (2nd edition). New York: Norton.

Feldman, F. (2004). *Pleasure and the good life: Concerning the nature, varieties, and plausibility of hedonism.* Oxford, UK: Oxford University Press.

Fishbein, M., & Ajzen, I. (1975). *Belief, attitude, intention, and behavior: An introduction to theory and research.* Reading, MA: Addison-Wesley.

Fredricksen, J., Wilhelm, J., & Smith, M. W. (2012). *So, what's the story?: Narrative writing to understand ourselves, others, and the world.* Portsmouth, NH: Heinemann.

Freud, S. (1913). *The interpretation of dreams.* (A. A. Brill, Trans.). New York: Macmillan. (Original work published in 1900)

Frijda, N. (2001). The nature of pleasure. In J. A. Bargh & D. K. Apsley (Eds.), *Unraveling the complexities of social life: A festschrift in honor of Robert B. Zajonc* (pp. 71–94). Washington, DC: American Psychological Association.

Frye, N. (1957). *Anatomy of criticism: Four essays.* Princeton, NJ: Princeton University Press.

Gerard, C. (2013). Retrieved from www.cindygerard.com January 5, 2013.

Goldbrunner, J. (1965). *Individuation: A study of the depth psychology of Carl Gustav Jung.* Notre Dame, IN: Notre Dame Press.

Gray, P. (March 20, 2000). Passion on the pages. *Time.* Retrieved from http://www.time.com/time/magazine/article/0,9171,996381,00.html

Greenblatt, S. (2011). *The swerve: How the world became modern.* New York: Norton.

Haidt, J. (2006). *The happiness hypothesis: Finding modern truth in ancient wisdom.* New York: Basic Books.

Hallie, P. (1969). *The paradox of cruelty.* Middletown, CT: Wesleyan University Press.

Harding, D. W. (1967). Considered experience: The invitation of the novel. *English in education, 1*(2), 8-9.

Hatlan, B. (1988). The return of the repressed/oppressed in Bram Stoker's *Dracula.* In M. Carter (Ed.), *Dracula: The vampire and the critics* (pp. 120-131). Ann Arbor, MI: UMI Research Press.

Heller, T. (1987). *The delights of terror: An aesthetics of the tale of terror.* Urbana, IL: University of Illinois Press.

Hirsch, E. D. (1987). *Cultural literacy: What every American needs to know.* Boston: Houghton Mifflin.

Hyder, S. (2001). *The wound of wisdom, the wisdom of the wound: Reflections on the vampire.* (Unpublished thesis). C.G. Jung Institute, Zurich.

Jobs for the Future. Connecting literacy and work. Retrieved from http://www.jff.org/projects/current/workforce/connecting-literacy-and-work/918

Johnson, R. (1983). *We.* New York: Harper Collins.

Johnson, R. (1986). *Inner work.* New York: Harper and Row.

Johnson, R. (1989a). *He: Understanding masculine psychology.* Berkeley, CA: Mills House.

Johnson, R. (1989b). *She.* New York: Harper Collins.

Johnson, R. (1992). The vampire archetype. Speech given to the Jung Society, Jacksonville, FL. Retrieved from http://jungian.info/library.cfm?idsLibrary=7

Jung, C. (1914). On the importance of the unconscious in psychopathology. *Collected works,* Vol. III, London: Routledge & Kegan Paul.

Jones, E. (1931). *On the nightmare.* London: Hogarth Press and Institute of Psycho-Analysis.

Jung, E. & von Franz, M. L. (1960). *The grail legend.* Princeton, NJ: Princeton University Press.

Kareem, N. (April 18, 2008). It's Baaack: Sweet Valley High Redux. Retrieved from http://www.racialicious.com/2008/04/18/its-baaack-sweet-valley-high-redux/

Mayes, C. (2007). *Inside education: Depth psychology in teaching and learning.* Madison, WI: Atwood.

Mayes, C. (2010). *The archetypal hero's journey in teaching and learning.* Madison, WI: Atwood Publishing.

McCann, T., L., Johannessen, R., Kahn, E., and J. Flanigan. (2006). *Talking in class: Using discussion to enhance teaching and learning.* Urbana, IL: National Council of Teachers of English.

McKenna, M.C., Conradi, K., Lawrence, C., Jang, B. G., & Meyer, J. P. (2012). Reading attitudes of middle school students: Results of a U.S. survey. *Reading Research Quarterly, 47,* 283–306.

McEwan, C. (2012). *World enough and time: On creativity and slowing down.* Dublin, NH: Bauhan.

National Endowment for the Arts. (2004). Reading at risk: A survey of literary reading in America (Research Report No. 42). http://www.nea.gov/pub/readingatrisk.pdf.

National Endowment for the Arts. (2009). Reading on the rise: A new chapter in American literacy. http://www.nea.gov/research/readingonrise.pdf.

Neale, S. (1980). *Genre.* London: British Film Institute.

Nell, V. (1988). *Lost in a book: The psychology of reading for pleasure.* New Haven, CT: Yale University Press.

Nussbaum, M. (1990). *Love's knowledge: Essays on philosophy and literature.* New York: Oxford University Press.

Nystrand, M. with Gamoran, A., Kachur, R., & Prendergast, C. (1997). *Opening dialogue: Understanding the dynamics of language and learning in the English classroom.* New York: Teachers College Press.

Papyrinski, J. (2011). List of horror subgenres. Retrieved from http://joannaparypinski.com/2011/06/29/list-of-horror-subgenres/.

Pollard, D. (2005). *The romance novel: Literature of liberation.* Retrieved from http://howtosavetheworld.ca/2005/02/17/the-romance-novel-literature-of-liberation

Pollitt, K. (1991). Reading books, great or otherwise. *Harpers,* December, 34-37.

Rabinowitz, P. J. (1987). *Before reading: Narrative conventions and the politics of interpretation.* Ithaca, NY: Cornell University Press.

Rabinowitz, P. J., & Bancroft, C. (in press). Euclid at the core: Recentering literary education. *Style.*

Rabinowitz, P. J., & Smith, M. W. (1998). *Authorizing readers: Resistance and respect in the teaching of literature.* New York: Teachers College Press.

Radway, J. (1984). *Reading the romance: Women, patriarchy, and popular literature.* Chapel Hill, NC: University of North Carolina Press.

Radway, J. (1986). Reading is not eating: Mass-produced literature and the theoretical, methodological, and political consequences of a metaphor. *Book Research Quarterly, 2,* 7-29.

Raible, C. G. (1988). *Dracula*: Christian Heretic. In M. Carter (Ed.), *Dracula: The vampire and the critics* (p. 105). Ann Arbor, MI: UMI Research Press.

Rosenblatt, L. (1978). *The reader, the text, the poem.* Carbondale, IL: Southern Illinois University Press.

Schiefele, U., Schaffner, E., Möller, J., & Wigfield, A. (2012). Dimensions of reading motivation and their relation to reading behavior and competence. *Reading Research Quarterly, 47,* 427-463.

Senf, C. A. (1988). Dracula: The Unseen Face in the Mirror. In M. Carter (Ed.), *Dracula: The vampire and the critics* (pp. 94). Ann Arbor, MI: UMI Research Press.

Singer, J. (1988). Foreword. In D. Feinstein, & S. Krippner (Eds.). *Personal mythology: Using rituals, dream and imagination to discover your inner story.* Los Angeles, CA: Jeremy P. Tarcher.

Smith, M. W., & Connolly, B. (2005). The effects interpretive authority on classroom discussions of poetry: Lessons from one teacher. *Communication Education, 54,* 271-288.

Smith, M. W., & Wilhelm, J. (2002). *"Reading don't fix no Chevys": Literacy in the lives of young men.* Portsmouth, NH: Heinemann.

Smith, M. W., & Wilhelm, J. (2006). *Going with the flow.* Portsmouth, NH: Heinemann.

Smith, M. W. & Wilhelm, J. (2010). *Fresh takes on teaching literary elements: How to teach what really matters about character, setting, point of view, and theme.* New York: Scholastic.

Smith, M. W., Wilhelm, J., Fredricksen, J. (2012). *O, yeah?!: Putting argument to work both in school and out.* Portsmouth, NH: Heinemann.

Smith, M. W., & Young, J. (1995). Assessing secondary students' liking of short stories. *Journal of Educational Research, 89,* 14-22.

Tatum, A. (2009). *Reading for their life: (Re)building the textual lineages of African American adolescent males.* Portsmouth, NH: Heinemann.

Twitchell, J. (1985). *Dreadful pleasures: An anatomy of modern horror.* New York: Oxford University Press.

USA Today. (2012, February, 2012). Why do we need romance novels? Retrieved from http://books.usatoday.com/happyeverafter/post/2012-02-13/why-do-we-need-romance-novels-authors-have-answers/62.

Vinz, R. (1996). Horrorscapes (in)forming adolescent identity and desire. *Journal of Curriculum Theorizing, 12*(4), 14–26.

Vipond, R. & Hunt, R. (1984). Point-driven understanding: Pragmatic and cognitive dimensions of literary reading. *Poetics, 13,* 261-277.

Vygotsky, L. S. (1978). *Mind in society.* Cambridge, MA: Harvard University Press.

Wasson, R. (1988), The Politics of *Dracula.* In M. Carter (Ed.), *Dracula: The vampire and the critics* (pp. 19–23). Ann Arbor, MI: UMI Research Press.

Wendell, S. (2013). Retrieved from *sbsarah.com/.../everything-i-know-about-love-i-learned-from-romance-novels*

Wilhelm, J. (1995). Reading is seeing: Using visual response to improve the literary reading of reluctant readers. *Journal of Reading Behavior, 27,* 467–503.

Wilhelm, J. (2007). *Engaging readers and writers with inquiry.* New York: Scholastic.

Wilhelm, J. (2008). *You gotta BE the book: Teaching engaged and reflective reading with adolescents* (2nd ed). New York: Teachers College Press.

Wilhelm, J. (2012a). *Improving comprehension with think aloud strategies: Modeling what good readers do.* (2nd ed.). New York: Scholastic.

Wilhelm, J. (2012b). *Action strategies for deepening comprehension.* (2nd ed.). New York: Scholastic.

Wilhelm, J. (2012c). *Enriching comprehension with visualization* (2nd ed.). New York: Scholastic.

Wilhelm, J., Boas, E. & Wilhelm, P. J. (2009). *Inquiring minds learn to read and write: 50 problem-based literacy & learning strategies.* New York: Scholastic.

Wilhelm, J., & Edmiston, B. (1998). *Imagining to learn: Inquiry, ethics and integration through drama.* Portsmouth, NH: Heinemann.

Wilhelm, J., & Novak, B. (2011). *Teaching literacy for love and wisdom: Being the book and being the change.* New York: Teachers College Press.

Wilhelm, J., Smith, M. W., & Fredricksen, J. (2012). *Get it done!: Writing informational text to make things happen.* Portsmouth, NH: Heinemann.

Winnicott, D. W. (1971). *Playing and reality.* London: Tavistock Publications.